"I admire Dr. Moody's work in the introduction—her understanding of the current critical literature is very complete. She has done considerable work to understand the trajectory of Whipple's career, to bring to bear the writings of Maria Stewart, David Walker, and Sojourner Truth, who used similar means of marshaling the written word to achieve fame, an outcome that has so far eluded Eldridge; she has done research in many public records to verify Whipple's urgent plea for justice where injustice was served with regard to Eldridge's real property. Dr. Moody's careful work in the public records is an important contemporary supplement to the 1838 text."

—Caroline F. Sloat, retired Director of Book Publication,
American Antiquarian Society

"*Memoirs of Elleanor Eldridge* is a crucial document in expanding our understanding of nineteenth-century African American print culture. Not a freed slave, nor a convicted criminal, nor a religious convert, Elleanor Eldridge's two biographies came into print in the 1830s for a vastly different reason: Eldridge was an entrepreneur and property owner who successfully used the legal system to regain title to property that had been illegally taken from her. Joycelyn Moody's thorough and sensitive introduction to this republication of the 1838 edition of *Memoirs* helps readers situate this remarkable woman in the racial context of antebellum Providence, and in the process offers valuable insights into the practice of collaborative authorship."

—Paul J. Erickson, Director of Academic Programs,
American Antiquarian Society

MEMOIRS OF ELLEANOR ELDRIDGE

ReGENERATIONS

AFRICAN AMERICAN LITERATURE AND CULTURE

VOLUME THREE

Also in this series:

A Nickel and a Prayer: The Autobiography of Jane Edna Hunter
Edited by Rhondda Robinson Thomas

Hearts of Gold
J. McHenry Jones

Regenerations: African American Literature and Culture is a series devoted to reprinting editions of important African American texts that either have fallen out of print or have failed to receive the attention they deserve. *Regenerations* encourages research that develops and extends the understanding of African American literary and cultural history, while promoting regional and local research that represents the complex dynamics of African American experience.

For all books published in this series, we seek out texts with wide and varied appeal, and we seek out scholars who are committed to providing original research on the authors and texts. Each book in the series benefits from collaborations between experienced and emerging scholars and features strong biographical and historical introductions, full annotations when appropriate, and, when possible, an appendix with relevant materials by or about the author. We reprint texts exactly as originally published with no emendation or silent correction.

"[Regenerations: African American Literature and Culture] is a vital, exciting series that makes available neglected texts that can help us to rethink African American literary and cultural traditions."—Robert S. Levine, Distinguished Scholar-Teacher, University of Maryland

"[This] series expands the scholarly discussion about the ways in which such texts let us reconsider the field and insure that the books will be taught in the classroom and thereby be sustained for the next generation."—Sharon Harris, Director, Humanities Institute and Professor of English, University of Connecticut

SERIES EDITORS
John Ernest, Professor and Chair of English, University of Delaware
Joycelyn K. Moody, Sue E. Denman Distinguished Chair in American Literature,
    University of Texas at San Antonio.

Memoirs

of

ELLEANOR ELDRIDGE

Original text by

FRANCES HARRIET WHIPPLE

with ELLEANOR ELDRIDGE

Edited by Joycelyn K. Moody

WEST VIRGINIA UNIVERSITY PRESS

MORGANTOWN 2014

West Virginia University Press, Morgantown 26506
©2014 by West Virginia University Press. All rights reserved.
Published 2014.

ISBN-13 (cloth) 978-1-935978-24-4
ISBN-13 (pb) 978-1-935978-23-7
ISBN-13 (epub) 978-1-935978-25-1
ISBN-13 (pdf) 978-1-938228-64-3

Library of Congress Cataloging-in-Publication Data

Green, Frances H. (Frances Harriet), 1805-1878.
Memoirs of Elleanor Eldridge / original text by Frances Harriet
Whipple, with Elleanor Eldridge; edited by Joycelyn K. Moody. -- First
edition.
        pages   cm. -- (Regenerations: African American literature and
culture)
Originally published: 1838.
ISBN 978-1-935978-24-4 (cloth : alk. paper) -- ISBN 1-935978-24-1
(cloth : alk. paper) -- ISBN 978-1-935978-23-7 (pbk. : alk. paper)
-- ISBN 1-935978-23-3 (pbk. : alk. paper) -- ISBN 978-1-935978-25-1
(epub) -- ISBN 1-935978-25-X (epub) -- ISBN 978-1-938228-64-3
(pdf) -- ISBN 1-938228-64-2 (pdf)
1. Eldridge, Elleanor, 1785-1862 2. African American women--
Rhode Island--Providence--Biography. 3. African Americans--Rhode
Island--Providence--Biography. 4. Free blacks--Rhode Island--Prov-
idence--Biography. 5. African Americans--Rhode Island--Provi-
dence--Social conditions--19th century. 6. Providence (R.I.)--Race
relations. 7. Providence (R.I.)--Biography. I. Eldridge, Elleanor, 1784-
1845? II. Moody, Joycelyn, 1957- editor. III. Title.
F89.P99N44 2013
974.5'203092--dc23
[B]
2013022150

Book and cover design by Than Saffel
Text composed by Nathan Holmes
Cover image and frontispiece of original text courtesy of
American Antiquarian Society

Contents

CONTENTS *continued*

To William L. Andrews and Frances Smith Foster,

for paving the way and showing me how,

to Lorraine J. Martínez,

woman of color entrepreneur extraordinaire,

and to Tanecia & Tiffany, and Bianika and the J's.

J.K.M.

Acknowledgments

I am indebted to many persons who helped me with this project over the years of its development, some quite unknowingly, in significant and diverse ways. I extend sincere thanks to John Ernest and Carrie Mullen for their expert, devoted supervision of the *Regenerations* series and their careful attention to this contribution to it. Working with you continues to be among my most profound professional pleasures. I owe a great debt to the Special Collections librarian at Penn State who, in winter 1991, gave me the photocopy of the 1841 edition of *Memoirs of Elleanor Eldridge* I use almost daily. I am deeply sorry I cannot recall or uncover his name now, as he will only know through a chance encounter with this book that his gift of the text during my half-hour visit with him so transformed my life. I am grateful for the thoughtful attention I received over the years from historians and archivists in Providence, Rhode Island, including Barbara Barnes, Paul R. Campbell, C. Morgan Grefe, Doyin E. Joseph, Ray Rickman, Seth Rockman, and Andrew B. Smith, as well as reference librarians and archivists at the public and private institutions I visited across Rhode Island. In Massachusetts, I benefited over many years from the joyful and brilliant generosity of the archivists at the American Antiquarian Society, especially Caroline Sloat, Elizabeth Pope, Jaclyn Penny, Paul Erickson, and Andrew Bourque. Scholars in residence I encountered during my AAS research trips offered friendly, useful, and far-ranging conversations. The warm hospitality and stimulating exchange I enjoyed at Williams College provided me an opportunity to reflect on aspects of this project at a critical turning point; I thank you especially, Vincent J. Schleitwiler. Invitations to deliver the 2008 Gilbert Lecture at Southern Methodist University and for a 2009 Diversity Research Institute Senior Lecture at the University of Washington allowed me to receive instructive commentary from generous and intelligent colleagues. Thank you, too, my dear University of Washington friends, Angela B. Ginorio and Karen M. Gourd. The University of Texas at San Antonio has been my home institution during the critical years of research on this book. For their support and dedication, I thank Bridget Drinka, Andrew Holt, Sonja Lanehart, Sue McCray, Tara Schmidt, Deborah D. Thomas, and Linda Winterbottom. All of my doctoral students shaped the project in important ways, and inspired me to work with discipline and mindfulness; my dissertation students Erin Ranft, Liz Cali, and Allegra Castro specifically urged me to model my best writing self. The expertise and excitement of Juli McLoone and also Jillian Walker, whom I met in the last season of this project's preparation, made all the difference.

My support network of intellectuals and loving friends sustained me across the years; thank you, Elizabeth Ammons; Kimberly Blockett; members of the National Center for Faculty Development and Diversity's Faculty Support Program during spring and summer 2012 (especially Kerry Ann Rockquemore, Lorraine Cordeiro, Roxanne Donovan, and Riyad Shajahan); P. Gabrielle Foreman; DoVeanna S. Fulton; Eric Gardner; Sue Mendelssohn; Barbara Neely; Howard Rambsy II; Sarah S. Robbins; Xiomara Santamarina; Christie L. Taylor and Katherine Mighty; and Priscilla Wald together with the staff and editorial board of *American Literature*. To those scholars and friends I have neglected to name here, please know I am very grateful despite my faulty memory. From my father, George Moody, Jr., I gained a valued model of discipline and perseverance. Finally, for their faithful and nurturing encouragement, come what may, I offer loving gratitude to my partner Lorraine J. Martínez, my son Patrick J. McDaniel, and my mother Catherine E. Moody. May *Memoirs of Elleanor Eldridge* ever inspire my beloved nieces—Tanecia Armstrong, Tiffany Shuford, Bianika Moody McClain, Jasmine Michele Davis, and Jada Adrianne Davis.

Introduction

> There are some adventitious circumstances which minister so
> directly to the necessities of the occasion, as almost brings a
> conviction that they are providential . . . and it seemed, really, as if a
> special Providence smiled upon her love.
>
> —*Memoirs of Elleanor Eldridge*[1]

> If a biography is not true it is worthless.
>
> —Edward H. O'Neill[2]

Why reclaim a biography that names no author on its title page for
a book series devoted to the recovery of African American literature
and culture? Why reprint now a biography by an antebellum white
woman that narrates the life of an obscure woman of mixed-race heritage? Who was Elleanor Eldridge, and what makes her life worth recovering today? This reprint of the first edition of *Memoirs of Elleanor
Eldridge* makes available a biography rarely encountered now, in spite
of it once having been sufficiently in demand to warrant two editions
and multiple reprints.[3] In fact, the *National Union Catalog of Pre-1956
Imprints* indicates that an edition of either *Memoirs of Elleanor Eldridge*
or *Elleanor's Second Book* was published every year between 1838 and
1847 (with the apparent exception of 1844); in some years, editions of
both biographies were reprinted for sale.[4] No new editions of *Memoirs
of Elleanor Eldridge* appeared after 1840, and the biography was not
reprinted again until the second half of the twentieth century, when

a broadly defined black power movement looked to the US historical past for notable figures of African descent.[5] Similarly, during the women's movement of the 1980s, the Eldridge biographies were excerpted in such groundbreaking anthologies as Dorothy Sterling's *We Are Your Sisters* (1984) and cited in accounts of African American women's history such as Darlene Clark Hine and Kathleen Thompson's *A Shining Thread of Hope* (1998).[6] The erratic regard paid to *Memoirs of Elleanor Eldridge* suggests the importance of Xiomara Santamarina's caution against "suppos[ing] that black authors' own audiences and historical eras were solely responsible for their erasure from the literary record: Sometimes when [black women's] texts appear, they fall by the critical wayside if they do not meet the requirements of what currently circulates as critical capital."[7] Even more, we should embrace John Ernest's declaration of the African American-ness of (auto)biographical texts of the nineteenth century, including those authored by white writers: the "blackness" of these texts is recoverable and "can be discovered in the complex interplay of the accounts of various individual lives, in the digressions that indicate a story beyond the clean lines of the promised plot, and in the stylistic roughness that suggests truths that do not quite fit into the discursive conventions and possibilities of the time."[8] In the case of *Memoirs of Elleanor Eldridge*, the tensions and interstices of this collaborative biography attest to the *racially* marginalized status and assertive identity of one of its coauthors.

This reprinted edition restores Eldridge to public attention and to the black sociopolitical and cultural contexts of mid-1800s Rhode Island not because such contexts are currently, or once more, in vogue—they are not—but because consistent, albeit shifting, attention to Eldridge's life story affirms its enduring importance to African Americans.[9] This interest has been constant since 1838, regardless of the critical capital circulating most urgently in any given era. By situating Eldridge in African American social history, I do not mean to oversimplify Eldridge's complex ethnic heritage(s) as the daughter of an indigenous mother and a black African father. Nor do I mean to reify the white supremacist model of Rhode Island legislators who, at whim, identified her multiple ethnic heritages—and that of many generations of other people born of a combination of indigenous, African, and/

or European parents or ancestors—by such terms as *colored, mustee, mulatto,* and over time, reductively *black.*[10] As Joanne Pope Melish reports, "By the beginning of the American Revolution, black, Indian, and mixed race slaves and servants as a group were often characterized as simply 'black'—'blackened' by their common servitude—and this characterization was beginning to be applied by whites to people of color of all sorts whether or not they had been enslaved or indentured. . . . By the 1770s, whites often referred to many [Narragansett] people collectively as 'black' or 'coloured' as well."[11] This reprint edition aims not to reconstruct colonial Rhode Island's racist white-nonwhite binary or to ignore Eldridge's indigenous ancestry but rather to trace sociohistorical factors that render her especially important to the history of African Americans—or, "blacks"—born free in the first years following Rhode Island emancipation. A relatively conservative legislature enacted a gradual end to slavery in Rhode Island, decreeing "all slaves born after 1 March 1784 were free, though it mandated that these children would remain under the control of their mothers' owners until their twenty-first birthday."[12] In any case, it is difficult to separate Eldridge's African and indigenous histories and cultural traits from one another because the written historical record, of which *Memoirs of Elleanor Eldridge* is part, does not detail such distinctions. Ultimately, persons seeking to know which indigenous ways and rites Eldridge practiced must face difficult work, for they necessarily find themselves in the paradoxical situation of looking in archival records for data deliberately omitted from state documents as unimportant and unworthy of preservation.[13]

Eldridge descended on both sides from people who at some point in their lives owned significant land or real estate. Her Native American and African American heritages are both loosely reconstructed in *Memoirs of Elleanor Eldridge*, but neither in sufficient detail to illuminate the politics of dual heritage or to enable ethnographic considerations of her complex subject location.[14] To an extent, the biographical subject is rendered palatable to white readers, her nonwhite racial identity depicted in terms designed not to threaten white readers. To the degree that white readers were taking a chance by permitting the nonwhite Eldridge to enter their homes as print culture, they were rewarded with her demurred racialized differences, her whitelike-ness. In the words of the narrator, "Elleanor Eldridge, on the one hand, is the inheritress of African blood, with all its heirship of wo [sic]; and the subject of wrong and banishment, by her Indian maternity on the other. Fully and sadly, have these titles been redeemed. It seems, indeed, as if the wrongs and persecutions of both races had fallen upon Elleanor."[15] The narrator of *Memoirs* asserts that the family of Mary Fuller, Eldridge's maternal foremother, "once held great possessions in large tracts of land; with a portion of which Mary Fuller purchased her husband Thomas Fuller, who, until his marriage, had been a slave."[16] In addition, although Elleanor's father, Robin Eldridge, was deprived of the land promised to him for service in the American Revolution, he eventually "became able to purchase land and build a small house"[17] with Elleanor's mother.

Throughout *Disowning Slavery*, Joanne Pope Melish examines a variety of immoral means by which Euro-American Rhode Islanders in the state's early history legislated the end of slavery but also simultaneously disowned their complicity with the institution, asserting tacitly that Rhode Island citizens had never treated Africans and their descendants in dehumanizing, demoralizing, and destructive ways. Furthermore, the early national state reasoned that if its black residents were unhappy with their social or political condition, the latter was the natural effect of innate African inferiority, and Euro-Americans bore no responsibility for black progress or the lack of it.

By the 1830s, Rhode Island constructed its nonwhite racial category for people descended both from precolonial American lands and from Africa. Continuing early settlers' divisions of English immigrants from others, they developed racial mythologies that, over time, as Jack D. Forbes notes, replaced ethnic diversity and pluralism with a white-non-white binary.[18] Furthermore, during and after the slave trade era, Rhode Island's elite deployed three identificatory terms: "negroes, mulattoes, and colored" to reference people of color.[19] In other words, state officials consistently refused to recognize Native Americans by their particular tribal names.[20]

Memoirs of Elleanor Eldridge is a biography written by Frances Harriet Whipple, or more precisely the product of collaboration between Whipple and her eponymous subject.[21] *Memoirs*, first printed in 1838 by B. T. Albro in Providence, Rhode Island, and a companion text, *Elleanor's Second Book*, first printed in 1839, were both expressly written to raise funds for lawsuits centered on Eldridge's real estate property in the 1830s.[22] The production of just one of these texts was a major feat. All the more significant, then, is the accomplishment of multiple editions of *Memoirs of Elleanor Eldridge* and *Elleanor's Second Book*, which attest to Eldridge's valor and perseverance in spite of extremely oppressive conditions. The story that each biography tells is remarkable for a variety of reasons that together warrant the reissue of Eldridge's life story.[23]

Although Eldridge is mentioned in a few social histories of New England published since the second half of the twentieth century, *Memoirs of Elleanor Eldridge* and *Elleanor's Second Book* rarely appear in literary studies that focus on any aspect of US women's writing, early African American writing, or New England literary history. Significantly, this edition of the 1838 *Memoirs* restores its original import: it clearly acknowledges Eldridge's involvement in the Rhode Island legal system, which was provocative in that her lawsuits centered on land dispossession in a state notorious for the theft of land masses once owned by indigenous people and for fraudulently depriving US soldiers of color of acreages granted to them. Indeed, Eldridge's own father was promised eighty hectares (or 198 acres) in New York's Mohawk River Valley.[24] As Robert Cottrol argues, "To understand how doctrines evolved, and perhaps more importantly, how law behaved, requires [us to develop] a sophisticated understanding of social stratification, economic development, political power, intellectual fashion, religious fervor, and ethnic rivalry" across US history.[25] That the last known of Eldridge's lawsuits restored her property to her renders her a nineteenth-century woman of African descent no less worthy of our attention than the other well-known women of color who followed her, including Isabella Baumfree (later Sojourner Truth),[26] Lucy Ann Delaney, and Ida B. Wells, all of whom also became plaintiff and/or defendant in multiple US lawsuits.

Memoirs of Elleanor Eldridge should now be read widely because it makes possible more and better reading by and about nineteenth-century African Americans. I want to remedy what Frances Smith Foster and Kim D. Green have observed about scholarly and African

Americanist neglect of pre-1900 black texts: "In neither [the Harlem Renaissance nor the Black Arts era] were pre-twentieth-century creative license, aesthetic experiments, complicated racial politics, and class distinctions deemed worthy of serious consideration."[27] As the life narrative of an African and indigenous woman coauthored with a white woman, *Memoirs of Elleanor Eldridge* illuminates interracial relations among free women in antebellum New England. We need not accept as forever and lamentably lost biographies and mediated narratives that seem to render "subaltern" subjects voiceless. Even bearing in mind Eve Allegra Raimon's caution that "the researcher experiences an inevitable moment of frustration or disappointment over the impossibility of knowing more," reading *Memoirs of Elleanor Eldridge* within the constructs and constraints of Eldridge's own era enables our deeper appreciation of recovered, remembered texts across the full reach of US interethnic literary and social history.[28]

Memoirs of Elleanor Eldridge tells a story remarkable in a number of ways. Primarily, *Memoirs of Elleanor Eldridge* chronicles the subject's life from her birth in 1785 through the year of the book's publication. The biography traces the postmemory of the forced transport of Eldridge's African grandparents from Zaire through the Middle Passage with their children.[29] One of their three sons, Robin Eldridge (?–1814), served as a Revolutionary War soldier.[30] He outlived his spouse Hannah Prophet (1744–1790), Elleanor's mother, who was of indigenous heritage; she died when Elleanor was about five years old.[31] Elleanor became an indentured adolescent; as such, she gained numerous lucrative domestic skills. *Memoirs* describes the young Eldridge as a "belle" attractive to men in her social milieu. The biography even includes four letters, purportedly from a sailor kinsman with whom she was in love for several years. After his death, Eldridge amassed enough wealth as a self-employed worker in Providence, Rhode Island, that by 1820 she had purchased real estate, first at 22 Spring Street in Ward 6 on the northern reaches of Providence and later more land elsewhere in Providence and Warwick, Rhode Island.[32] She erected houses on her land and leased them to tenants. By 1838, Rhode Island tax records would—under the heading "People of Color"—identify her as paying twenty dollars in real estate taxes; put another way, that year—and for the next twenty—Eldridge held the greatest amount of personal wealth among women of color and was the third wealthiest person among black people.[33] She was defrauded of her property in 1835, but an 1838 court restored her property to her.

The amanuensis and narrator of *Memoirs of Elleanor Eldridge* expresses protofeminist outrage at the powerful (male) "extortioners" who caused Eldridge's loss and distress, and as an apprentice writer, Whipple uses her sentimentalized crafting of Eldridge's life story as an opportunity to hone the professional skills she would apply to more than a dozen other books under her byline throughout the second half of the nineteenth century.[34] For her part, Eldridge's participation in the biography demonstrates her honoring what DoVeanna S. Fulton (later Fulton Minor) calls "Black women's tradition of 'testifying' to experience as resistance to injustice," in Eldridge's case, to white supremacist and patriarchal legal infringements on her reputation and her property.[35] In short, Eldridge and Whipple each had significant reasons to collaborate on *Memoirs*, and both reaped life-changing rewards from their endeavor and product.

Memoirs of Elleanor Eldridge and Nineteenth-Century Interracial Coauthorship

> In interpretative biography the writer is attempting to present not only the physical but the mental aspects of his subject, and it is in that attempt that many biographers stumble into the numerous pitfalls that line their paths.
>
> —Edward H. O'Neill[36]

> It seems to me that the beauty of biography consists in simplicity, clearness, and brevity. I wish to give faithful portraits of individuals, and leave my readers in freedom to analyse their expression.
>
> —Lydia Maria Child[37]

> Ellen has traits of character, which, if she were a white woman, would be called *noble*. And must color so modify character that they really are not so?
>
> —Frances Whipple[38]

What kind of biography is *Memoirs of Elleanor Eldridge*? How does it compare with life narratives by and/or about other people of African descent—free or enslaved—produced during the same era? What does the biography insinuate about the (in)stability of power relations in Eldridge and Whipple's collaboration? What does it indicate about the complexities of white (women's) rhetorical representations of women (of color) biographical subjects? What complications arise in *Memoirs of Elleanor Eldridge* as the "illiterate" woman exerts control over the material outcome of her biography through subversive dialogue with her amanuensis?

Memoirs of Elleanor Eldridge shares many of the compelling concerns of other texts in which a white liberal or sympathetic amanuensis inscribes an illiterate subjugated narrator.[39] Collaborative writing teams comprised of a white person and an African-indigenous woman pose particular scholarly challenges in examinations of literary production.[40] For example, attending more to Eldridge than to Whipple has proven ironically difficult in that biographers generally strive to disappear from the biographies they craft. In addition, western paradigms in the academy and beyond have long privileged written words over oral words and spoken discourse, though in recent years, literary critics have increasingly observed this inequity. Particularly useful is Fulton's important scholarship, which astutely aligns "Black feminist orality [with] the African American women's tradition of 'sass' in which one responds with independence, knowing, and force to an individual in authority. . . . Black feminist orality is a more abstract notion with features of circularity and multiplicity that counter the hegemony of writing."[41] In that vein, rather than revisit the social conditions that privileged Whipple's access to writing and academic education over Eldridge's, this introduction reconstructs Eldridge's relationship to literacy. More aggressively, it analyzes the conditions of her life that made her a complex biographical subject; as a class-defined and class-inflected genre, biography more conventionally addresses a wealthy and/or (in)famous person who readily claims public attention.

Interracial writing dyads were common in the early nineteenth century for a variety of reasons, including whites' greater access to publishers and to the acquisition of conventional writing skills. Scholarly prioritizing of this white privilege has overlooked a key concept of authorial power: stories are the foundation of written discourse in English—what is written is generally storytelling—and, therefore, English speakers possess some of the essential tools to communicate, to narrativize in English even when they do not possess writing skills. The significant number of interracial writing projects did not protect interracial writing collaborations from the white supremacist tensions that permeated all social life in the United States then. Complications of mediated or collaborative interracial narratives at the beginning of the nineteenth century arose from gaps in differentially raced experiences, yielding miscommunication and misunderstandings even when a white writer had the best of intentions to partner faithfully with a writer of color.[42] In addition, the era's white supremacist patriarchy yielded final editorial and ideological control over the written product more to white writers than to people of color.[43]

Because interracial collaborative writing of the era generally reveals the competing and oppositional discourses that emerge in such writing situations, we should heed DoVeanna Fulton's and Jean Humez's claims for regarding the writing dyad as coauthors.[44] By separate turns, these feminist critics extend William L. Andrews's earlier discussion of the naïve and negrophobic perception of "the black first-person narrator [as] a shallow intellectual vessel whose capacity would be strained by more than the oral relation of simple facts about his life."[45] Humez specifically argues to replace *dictated* as a frequent signifier of multiple-author autobiographies with *facilitated* or *mediated*, and contends that "a close analysis of the mediated text can help us speculate in an informed way about how the storyteller exercised significant control over aspects of the life-history text that was ultimately produced out of the collaboration."[46] Tacitly responding to calls like Humez's for "a new conception of the mediated life-story text and new textual analysis techniques," Fulton theorizes the politics and development of black women's orality; she defines such orality "as a speech act that resists or subverts oppression, and controls representations, thereby substantiating subjectivity."[47] Fulton cogently asserts that orality in texts by African Americans "illustrates an alternative epistemology that affirms Black subjectivity without restricting identity," and locates "the political nature of orality . . . in resistance to domination and dehumanization [and] its validation of African American culture and communities as significant to the development of self-determined, self-defined subjects."[48] Moreover, Shoshana Felman contends that testifying entails not only narration but also "comit[ting] oneself" to narrative, other persons, and a historical occurrence with its consequences.[49] Applying these theories to Eldridge and Whipple's collaborative relationship highlights Eldridge's contributions to narratives that could not exist without her participation. Although Eldridge's kin and sociopolitical communities are not centered in *Memoirs of Elleanor Eldridge*, allusions to them suggest her insistence on their importance in her life—as well as perhaps her protection of them from Whipple's unblinking gaze and intrusion.

Identifying *Memoirs* as a *coauthored* biography, I mean to respond to DoVeanna Fulton Minor's appeal that scholars give the literariness of African Americans' mediated narratives the same close critical attention they have generally reserved for the rhetorical devices of written slave narratives: such critical "concentration," in her words, "obscures and dismisses the significance of oral slave narratives as texts *authored* by their narrators."[50] Fulton Minor further theorizes black women's orality using the narratives of three formerly enslaved women—Louisa Picquet, Mattie J. Jackson, and Silvia Dubois (whose mediated life narratives were published in 1861, 1866, and 1883, respectively)—to contend that these "three women display conscious narrative power: the power of experiential testimony, oral manifestation, and commitment to and demand for justice by African American women. Without the benefits and privilege of reading and writing literacy (and in collaboration, sometimes uneasy, with amanuenses), these women left documents of their lives and of the challenges of African American women to make their voices heard."[51] Narrative negotiations between Eldridge and Whipple are apparent throughout *Memoirs*, as Whipple self-consciously warns readers against misreading Eldridge's story as "fictitious," for its subject "is none the less a *heroine* because it [the story] is *true*"—for all her deployment of tropes conventionally reserved for "marvellous [*sic*] tales."[52]

Even recognizing Eldridge's orality, we must confront the validity of Frances Smith Foster's claims in "Creative Collaboration: As African

American as Sweet Potato Pie."[53] Foster persuasively demonstrates that antebellum US black writers were not all victimized by interracial collaborations; early nineteenth-century *intraracial* collaboration predominated in many forums, including antislavery reading rooms, the Prince Hall Masons, lyceums, reading societies, church groups, the earliest black schools, and mutual aid societies like those formed by William J. Brown, another black and indigenous Providence resident during the years Eldridge lived there.[54] Such institutions are central to Elizabeth McHenry's *Forgotten Readers: Recovering the Lost History of African American Literary Societies*, which "argues that African American literary societies were formed not only as places of refuge for the self-improvement of the members but as acts of resistance to the hostile racial climate that made the United States an uncomfortable and unequal place for all black Americans, regardless of social or economic conditions."[55] In the eighteenth century, models of intraracial writing collaboration included legal documents, such as the 1783 and 1787 petitions for reparations made to the state of Massachusetts by an elder named Belinda enslaved for over fifty years by Loyalist Isaac Royall of Medford; because of his own petition to the Massachusetts state legislature for citizenship rights at the same time, social activist and Masons founder Prince Hall is thought to have provided editorial assistance with Belinda's petitions.[56] Such petitions, as David N. Gellman notes, "contradicted the mocking dialect-driven anecdotes" written by white abolitionists and, while deploying rhetorical tools other than sentimental poetry, also "prefigured in prose form antislavery poetry published in New York" and around New England. "Thus," Gellman continues, "blacks claimed their own voice consistent with their view of equality" as they entered the public sphere and seized print articulations of black voices that whites appropriated for public documents.[57]

Compared to intraracial writing dyads who produced postbellum US slave narratives, Eldridge's relationship to Whipple seems dramatically different. *Memoirs* might be contrasted with such texts as the *Story of Mattie J. Jackson*, by Lucy Susan Thompson, an account of a freed woman's life that deploys the tropes of antebellum black autobiography (even though it appeared in 1866, just *after* the ratification of the December 1865 Thirteenth Amendment). An example of an extant autobiography by ex-slavewomen, this narrative resulted from collaboration between two black women related by marriage and covers the intricate interstices of convoluted legal relationships surrounding African Americans and legal marriage.[58] In light of burgeoning research on nineteenth-century black intraracial collaborations in the United States, it is all the more intriguing that, in spite of opportunities for producing her life story with another person of color in 1830s Providence, Eldridge coauthored *Memoirs of Elleanor Eldridge* with Whipple.

Collaboration between people of color and white writers was not uncommon in New England by 1838, the year *Memoirs of Elleanor Eldridge* was first published, but more often the texts that such collaboration produced were formulated as captivity narratives or colonial or antebellum slave narratives.[59] Interracial collaboration had been a mode of telling black life long before 1838—and most featured an enslaved person.[60] *Memoirs of Elleanor Eldridge* exhibits features that would become classic in antebellum slave narratives—life stories of fugitive (that is, self-emancipated) or formerly enslaved persons— such as Harriet Jacobs's anonymously published *Incidents in the Life of a Slave Girl, Written by Herself* (1861). As I have outlined elsewhere such features included paratexts written by whites to validate the black narrator's authenticity and honor; scenes of familial loss and other traumas; valuations of Euro-American literacy and epistemologies; and meditations on sociopolitical and socioeconomic injustices.[61] Although Eldridge was never enslaved, her biography nevertheless forms a pioneering text in the literature of slavery. So thoroughly does *Memoirs* incorporate tropes of slave narratives published before it that David Quigley and Paul Finkelman mislabel it as "one of the earliest slave narratives by a woman."[62]

Among other same-gender interracial collaborations like Eldridge and Whipple's is *A Narrative of the Life and Adventures of Venture [Smith], a Native of Africa*. Transcribed by Connecticut schoolteacher Elisha Niles and published in 1798, it narrates an account of Smith's life of brutal involuntary servitude primarily on Fisher's Island, off the Connecticut coast.[63] Venture Smith had arrived as a child captive aboard the slaver *Charming Susanna* in Rhode Island—the state in which Eldridge was born free in 1785—from Anomabu, West Africa, by way of Barbados.[64] Smith's *Narrative* describes his acquisition of skills in diverse trades, his business success and eventual self-purchase, and his purchases of his spouse and their children, as well as his acquisitions of extensive property in East Haddam, Connecticut.[65] Both Smith and Eldridge pursued what would in the twentieth century be regarded as middle-class respectability as they fashioned themselves morally scrupulous and financially frugal among white New Englanders; they pursued economic self-reliance in an era that sought to restrict financial solvency to white men born into generations of wealth. Like the narrative apparatus of Smith's *Narrative*, that of *Memoirs of Elleanor Eldridge* contains what William L. Andrews calls a "pathetic element" accentuating Eldridge's "endurance, not active heroism."[66] The collaborative relationship between Smith and Niles parallels Eldridge's with Whipple in that each used a white amanuensis to publish their life stories, and both navigated the political landscape in New England to gain the economic, social, and political capital needed to purchase real estate. Both Niles and Whipple explain that the respective narratives are incomplete: whereas Whipple announces that Eldridge withheld details about her adolescent romances, Niles acknowledges in his preface to Smith's *Narrative* that he "omitted" some details to keep the text concise.[67] Niles and Whipple regarded their coauthors as needful and inferior victims; both biographies grieve what their narrative subjects might have become, ironically undercutting the print accounts of their actual accomplishments.[68] Moreover, both Smith and Eldridge unabashedly participated in the New England marketplace, even to collaboration with their respective interlocutors and engagement with publishers for the promulgation of their stories as material books to be sold. Surely, such decisions were as brave as they were shrewd.

Departing from virtually every other interracially produced text of that era, including the well-known *Interesting Narrative of the Life of Olaudah Equiano, or Gustavus Vassa, the African* (1791), neither Smith's book nor Eldridge's endorses Christianity, and neither narrates a conversion to Christian faith.[69] The explicit religious mores in *Memoirs of Elleanor Eldridge* derive more from contemporaneous tropes of sentimental and abolitionist rhetoric than from any implied or expressed Christian devotion practiced by either Eldridge or Whipple. (The religious tropes of convenience in *Memoirs* arguably have more in common with those of *Our Nig*, written some twenty years later by Harriet E. Wilson, another free, northern-born woman whose mixed-race ancestry included African foreparents.[70]) Notably, Christianity does not form a significant theme in B. B. Thatcher's *Memoir of Phillis Wheatley* either.[71] Wheatley was already deceased when Benjamin Thatcher wrote *Memoir of Phillis Wheatley, a Native African and a Slave* (1834), and nothing in the biography suggests that she collaborated with Thatcher before her death to produce it.

Conversely, *History of Mary Prince, a West Indian Slave, Related by Herself*, does recount its eponymous West Indian subject's conversion to Christianity and her eventual manumission.[72] Produced in London in 1831 by British "editors" and white amanuenses Susanna Strickland and Thomas Pringle, Prince's *History* has been labeled "a founding narrative in the canons of African Atlantic writing in English."[73] As secretary of the Anti-Slavery Society in London, Pringle would have been familiar with accounts of bondage; the anxiety about slavery's sexual violence that Prince disclosed is apparent in the numerous authenticating paratexts that threaten to overwhelm the pamphlet that contains the formerly enslaved woman's reconstruction of her bound life.[74] Furthermore, *History of Mary Prince* documents the violence, hard labor, and forced migration Prince endured after being sold multiple times to increasingly sadistic slaveholders. Just as Eldridge was both defendant and plaintiff in Rhode Island courts in the late 1820s and early 30s, Mary Prince "testif[ied] before the London Court of Common Pleas in a suit brought by Pringle against Thomas Cadell of *Blackwoods Magazine*, on 21 February 1833."[75] In addition, a struggle for narrative control is evident in both *Memoirs of Elleanor Eldridge* and *History of Mary Prince*, though Whipple never promises, as do Pringle and Strickland, to retain Eldridge's voice in the biography. However, *Memoirs* contains nothing close to the documentation of psychosexual sadism described graphically in *History of Mary Prince*; indeed even the impassioned decries of the racism and sexism Eldridge suffered bear no resemblance to the sordid details on every page of Prince's *History*.

Although *Memoirs of Elleanor Eldridge* does not specify how Whipple and Eldridge came to know each other or with which collaborator the idea for the biography originated, it reveals from the preface forward significant if also subtle aspects of Whipple and Eldridge's collaboration. The first sentence of the 1838 preface establishes the narrative perspective as other than Eldridge's since she, it becomes clear, is referenced as "suffering and persecuted merit."[76] Moreover, the preface begins demurely by identifying the biography as a "little book . . . to be published for the express purpose of giving a helping hand" to the biographical subject. Tacitly, the synecdoche "helping hand" reminds readers of the material object they hold to touch—that is, physically handle and manipulate, in the most literal sense—and ostensibly to aid (the life of) the black and indigenous woman subject. Further, "helping hand" connotes both the exchange of goods, mercantile trade, but it also underscores Eldridge's biography as a commodity: a material, cultural, social, political, and economic artifact that claims a particular place not only in the capital city's marketplace but also in New England's influential and various print culture contexts of the era. Ironically, an absence of personal pronouns overdetermines the first two sentences: to prioritize text, want, and worth, *neither* biographer nor subject is identified. Nonetheless, the "little book" of the first sentence assures readers of the modesty and propriety of both the writing woman and the speaking woman, a delicacy reinforced by the limits of their request for fiduciary assistance as "some little assistance" to imperiled merit. The graceful manners of the "writer" in particular are corporeally reiterated in the closing paragraph's allusion to conventional (white) female fragility, when she "crave[s] the indulgence of Elleanor's patrons" for any errors in the text that might be the result of her striving to finish writing the narrative "during a season of severe ilness, which has completely unfitted her for any exertion."[77]

Ultimately, though, the first person singular "writer of these *Memoirs*" announces in the preface to *Memoirs of Elleanor Eldridge* her motivation of seeking to aid Eldridge, and—or by—seeking readers who will "alleviate the misfortune" and provide solace to "suffering and persecuted merit."[78] Even though *merit* serves to esteem Eldridge, the self-designated "writer" thus proclaims for herself from the outset a greater measure of narrative power and authorial control than she recognizes in her needful collaborator. Literally wielding the pen, she implies, empowers her, further, to imagine and set a second, related goal: "bringing forward, and setting before the colored population, an example of industry and untiring perseverance, every way worthy their regard and earnest attention."[79] Invoking the non-self-referential pronoun *their*, the writer separates herself both from "the colored population," and in the succeeding sentence, from those "numerous friends and patrons of poor Elleanor, [who] are confident that the feeling and humane . . . will cheerfully subscribe for her book." Asserting this juxtaposition from conventional authorial height and presumed omniscience, the narrator erects superior, racialized poles: on the one hand, *Memoirs* seeks to offer Eldridge as an exemplum of industry and "perseverance" to lead the "colored population" to assimilation, emulation, virtue, and wealth, and on the other hand, *Memoirs* would inspire the writer's own condescension in "the feeling and humane." In addition, the narrator uses pointed racialized and self-excluding discourse, musing, "Still further, it is to be believed that the colored people, generally, will be proud to assist in sustaining one, who is both an honor and an ornament to their race."[80] Thus the preface—ironically, it turns out—suggests a fixed, raced, absolute, socioeconomic class gap: either an individual is interested in helping the victimized and persecuted Elleanor, and has the will and resources to do so; or one is a member of "the colored population" (referred to three times in the 200-word preface) and needs to learn from her example and should be proud to assist Eldridge in regaining her economic footing. In short, the "writer of these *Memoirs*" suggests a racialized difference (if not division) between, on one hand, the "numerous friends and patrons of poor Elleanor" and, on the other hand, "the colored people" who could and should use her as an example of diligence and discipline.

As a collaborative text that invokes the oral and literary traditions circulating while Eldridge and Whipple worked together, *Memoirs of Elleanor Eldridge* not only constitutes a counter-discourse to early US narratives by (formerly) enslaved persons; it also integrates other popular genres in the early national era, including sentimental (and) domestic fiction for women. *Memoirs* combines the conventions of antebellum slave narratives, domestic fiction discourses, and conduct manuals, by early US (primarily Anglo American) women writers.

Typically didactic and editorial, *Memoirs* incorporates aphorisms from literary works ranging from Shakespeare to the Scriptures, citing on the title page, for example, an apt monologue from *The Merchant of Venice*:

O that estates, degrees, and offices,
Were not derived corruptly! and that clear honor
Were purchased by the merit of the wearer!
How many, then, should cover, that stand bare?
How many be commanded, that command? (II.ix.41–45)

From the outset, then, the biography condemns criminal land dispossession, especially at the hands of corrupt law enforcement. From this epigraph *Memoirs* proclaims itself an extraordinary story of honor, merit, and the purchase of estates, one that exposes shameful, corrupt commanders; it is, the epigraph suggests, a story exceptional precisely because its heroine is one of "clear honor" with nothing to hide.

As for words the biography attributes to Eldridge in "her own voice," the very first are the most memorable: "There was a young man—I *had* a cousin—He sent a great many letters."[81] Thus, Eldridge's initial represented speech, significantly rendered in putative Standard American English (as opposed to Whipple's construction of a local black dialect), demurely recalls a beau named Christopher G. Before these words, all assertions tied to Eldridge are inscribed in the narrator's first-person report of Eldridge's speech. The letters she references, addressed to Elleanor when she is in her late twenties, are among the biography's most remarkable features. Placed intermittently near the middle of the text, three of these letters are dated March 27, August 27, and November 20, 1805, respectively, with a fourth on June 30, 1811.[82] Christopher's letters are conventional expressions of what Pamela Newkirk calls "the rhapsody of romance." They validate Newkirk's claim that "African Americans of all economic classes have, throughout their history, risen above personal circumstance to forge and maintain bonds of affection."[83]

However, *Memoirs of Elleanor Eldridge* is *not* a seduction tale.[84] To maintain the implication that Eldridge was chaste throughout her life, the biographies suggest that the intimacy with Christopher never included coitus.[85] Referring to Christopher as a cousin further distances suggestions of physical sexual activity and thus protects

Eldridge's reputation as a virgin. Whipple borrows and blends tropes of the epistolary tradition and the seduction novel, with Eldridge emerging as more stalwart, discerning, admirable, and rational (versus primitive and hypersexualized), as compared to eponymous fallen figures in women's seduction and domestic fiction in early republic US literature for women, such as *Charlotte Temple* (1794) by Susanna Rowson, and Elizabeth Wharton (fictional analogue of the historical Eliza Whitman) in *The Coquette* (1797), a *roman à clef* by Hannah Foster that Whipple had likely read.[86] "Founded on Fact," as Hannah Foster proclaims in the subtitle of her fictional account in letters of Wharton's/Whitman's misfortunes, *Memoirs of Elleanor Eldridge* ironically exposes Whipple's authorial struggle for dominance in the biography. That is, because, Whipple asserts, Eldridge will divulge only a few details about her affective youth, Whipple can do no more than insinuate that the letters included in *Memoirs* are "founded on fact." The clear contest between Eldridge and Whipple for voice, power, privacy, and representation is one now familiar to readers of nineteenth-century African American literature, along with inquiries into antebellum US women's identity politics and "the differences in perspective between African American women who were survivors of slavery and their white political allies."[87] Of greater interest today are theorizations of the nature of collaboration and inquiries about the process of rhetorical negotiations involving and engaging multiple persons.

Whether or not Eldridge was familiar with the representations of psychosexual sadism that shaped readers' assessments of the moral character of the title figure of *History of Mary Prince*, published in London a mere six years before *Memoirs of Elleanor Eldridge*, she might have known of other women of color who had been consciously or naively betrayed by white amanuenses whom they trusted to publish their life stories. As it is, the sentimental tropes Whipple deploys in *Memoirs* depict Eldridge as simultaneously virginal, sexualized, and generally silent: a figure extraordinarily divergent from both elite white women like Hannah Foster's Elizabeth Whitman and enslaved women subjected to all manner of corporeal and psychological depravity. Whipple achieves this portrait of Eldridge, grown from attractive youth into modest maturity, by giving her virtually no voice at all in *Memoirs of Elleanor Eldridge*. Over and over, not Eldridge but the narrator reports how Eldridge negotiated with Miss Elleanor Baker, daughter of "Mr. Joseph Baker, of Warwick."[88] Likewise, Eldridge is reported as "making a definite Bargain with Miss Baker, before she consented to put herself under her protection, evincing, by this single act, a degree of prudence and wisdom entirely beyond her years. She fixed her price at 25 cents per week, and agreed to work for one year."[89] By using indirect discourse to illustrate Eldridge's business acumen, insight, negotiation skills, and self-determination, Whipple thus highlights the raced differences between a white woman dependent on her father and needful of his consent and intervention and a single woman of color who must and can take charge of her own life and enter the political economy, public sphere, and work force of necessity and with confidence. Nowhere in the text before this passage does *Memoirs* allude to Eldridge as a speaking subject. This report of Eldridge's express verbal authority is a powerful and complex rhetorical gesture, a speech act that endows the white woman narrator with rhetorical power borrowed from the woman of color negotiating for her livelihood.[90]

If one takes at face value the direct discourse attributed to Eldridge when revealing with a sigh that she "had a cousin," then Christopher's death at sea proves convenient for Whipple's portrayal of a prudent and virtuous black and indigenous woman who cannot—or, ironically, will not—tell her own life story. The narrator of *Memoirs* follows this divulgence with the lament that "not a syllable more could I ever extract from her."[91] Significantly, *Memoirs* contains no letters from Eldridge to this paramour, nor does it allude to another suitor.[92] Whipple's revelation of her attempt to penetrate the privacy Eldridge clearly insisted on maintaining demonstrates Raimon's contention that "the pervasive and constitutive element of coerced silence in nineteenth-century African American literature can hardly be understated or more central to any discussion of what is always already lacking in a writer's life and work."[93] Indeed, in the succeeding decade, Sojourner Truth would register her own "firm intention . . . early in the interview process [with Olive Gilbert] to censor some of her painful slavery experiences."[94]

Whipple's rhetorical choice to use a white woman analogue as the biography's narrator—rather than the more common first-person "colored" speaker of other black and indigenous life writings, both self-authored and told—suggests her reluctance to "leav[e] vocal pitch and pace to the [white] imagination" and her hesitation to enable her white readers "to dismiss the words without listening to or confronting the author."[95]

Frances Harriet Whipple, Eldridge's coauthor, was born in September 1805 into the fifth generation of the Whipple family of Smithfield, Rhode Island.[96] According to Sarah O'Dowd, Whipple's biographer, George Whipple (1776–1820), Frances's father, was one in a long line of "eminent, successful men"; in her childhood, the family had substantial wealth and thereby enjoyed the cultural and sociopolitical capital of elite white society and her parents' abundant social privileges.[97] Her mother, Ann Scott Whipple (who also went by Nancy), bore four other children before she died in 1823, when Frances was eighteen years old. By the time Ann died, George Whipple had already lost seven siblings, and in 1816 he sold away his share of his father's farm; thus, grief and land loss seem to have diminished his capacity to provide adequately for his family.[98] Still, as a child, Frances received a public education, and as a young woman, she "attended a private school in Providence, kept by Dr. Peter W. Ferris," circa 1832.[99] At age twenty-four, in May 1829 (the year that David Walker published his mighty *Appeal* in nearby Boston), Whipple began publishing a Providence periodical she called the *Original* as well as a series of temperance texts. In a biographical sketch of Whipple's professional career, Sidney Rider asserts that she intended to issue the *Original* three times each year, but only two numbers appeared: the first in May 1829, containing fifteen articles in over one hundred pages, ten articles of which she wrote herself, and the second in January 1830, running forty pages, and featuring "sketches of local interest."[100] As the unnamed author and narrator of *Memoirs of Elleanor Eldridge*, Whipple perhaps collaborated with Eldridge precisely because doing so afforded her a worthy occasion to rail against oppressions that had hindered her own intellectual and social growth. Later books Whipple published would protest sociopolitical maltreatment of poor people, people of color, and white women, that is, the most disenfranchised and vulnerable in the early United States. *Memoirs of Elleanor Eldridge* didactically argues for social propriety and patriotic duty. The particular lessons Eldridge and Whipple seem determined to teach—individually and collaboratively—turn on legal rights for subjugated dark-skinned ethnic minorities and national reform of academic training of women. To that end, it is no coincidence that their collaborative biographies of Eldridge's life and legal troubles dramatically underscore the twin notions of land and liberty as inextricable forces in the American imagination, and tacitly direct readers to fight vigorously to protect individual rights, especially those of the disenfranchised.

Whipple coauthored *Memoirs of Elleanor Eldridge* presumably as, in Rider's words, "a work of charity," yet most of Whipple's later books were the means by which she sought to earn an independent income.[101] The Juvenile Emancipation Society chose 1840 to publish a concise collection of antislavery poems and short stories for children, titled *The Envoy, From Free Hearts to the Free* and printed at Pawtucket by R. W. Potter.[102] No author-editor is named, but Rider identifies Whipple as both editor and contributor of several articles.[103] Potter was also the printer of a small volume distributed by the Ladies Anti-Slavery Society of Providence, titled *Liberty Chimes*, to which Whipple contributed.[104] In 1841, she published the novel *The Mechanic*, the first known book bearing her name as author on the title page. In 1842, she affiliated herself with Governor Thomas Dorr, and at age thirty-seven, she wed twenty-year-old Charles Green in Lowell, Massachusetts; according to O'Dowd, they divorced on September 20, 1847.[105] Also in 1842, Whipple became editor of a factory women's *Journal* in Massachusetts, and two years later, she published the prolabor novel titled *Might and Right*.[106] After her divorce from Green, Whipple moved among friends in New England, and in 1850 she entered the home of Universalist minister Samuel Byron Brittan, a spiritualist with whom she published spiritualist tracts.[107] She spent a very prolific decade with Brittan, writing, for example, a second biography: *Biography of Mrs. Semantha Mettler, the Clairvoyant: Being a History of Spiritual Development and Containing an Account of the Wonderful Cures Performed through Her Agency* (1853), as well as coauthoring with Joseph Whipple Congdon the *Analytical Class-Book of Botany, Designed for Academies and Private Students* (1855). She caught the figurative fever to go west, and made her way to San Francisco, where, in 1861, she married William C. McDougall. Rider reports Whipple's last known "literary labor" was *Beyond the Veil: Posthumous Work of Paschal Beverly Randolph, Aided by Emanuel Swedenborg and Others, through the Minds of Frances H. McDougall and Luna Hutchinson*, published in 1878.[108] On June 10, 1878, Frances Harriet McDougall died in Oakland, California.

Neither Eldridge nor Whipple was a mother, and though Eldridge apparently did not travel beyond New England, both women rejected long-term domesticity and rootedness in favor of self-determined mobility. Although Eldridge purchased property and leased out homes, she lodged in transient situations, evidently by choice; Whipple herself set the course of her migrations when married and not. Their collaborative writing projects parallel this propensity for self-empowerment, suggesting each woman perceived "that writing, especially print," as Grey Gundaker suggests, "gives words spatial and temporal mobility [perhaps] even . . . with social and cognitive revolutions."[109] Both women defied codes of true and republican motherhood, in part, no doubt, to protect themselves against the loss of real estate and personal property, which by eighteenth-century law transferred from wives to husbands when they married. William Blackstone's 1765 writing "Of Husband and Wife," for example, stipulates that "though our law in general considers man and wife as one person, yet there are some instances in which she is separately considered; as inferior to him, and acting by his compulsion. And therefore all deeds executed, and acts done, by her, during her coverture, are void, or at least voidable."[110] Whipple's mother had brought considerable wealth to her marriage, and after her death, her husband lost (interest in) not only his share in his own family's farm, but Ann's wealth as well. The impact of this loss diminished Whipple's social status as well as her opportunities for intellectual and professional advancement, so she would reasonably have felt an especial kinship with another woman who resisted men's authority and control of women's assets. Thus, Eldridge's story not only enabled Whipple's rebuttal of chauvinism, with limited risk to Whipple's own status as a white woman, but it also enabled her to pursue professional skills, with strategically little risk to her professional reputation since no edition of *Memoirs of Elleanor Eldridge* names its author.

Memoirs of Elleanor Eldridge, Sentimentalism, and (Black) Print Culture as (White) Women's Political Activism

> No MAN ever would have been treated so; and if A WHITE WOM-
> AN had been the subject of such wrongs, the whole town—nay, the
> whole country, would have been indignant: and the actors would
> have been held up to the contempt they deserve!
>
> —*Memoirs of Elleanor Eldridge*[111]

Why did Eldridge and Whipple choose a book, and specifically (black) print culture contexts, as their means of protest against the system that threatened Eldridge's property? What rhetorical and moral advantages did Eldridge and Whipple gain by choosing a sentimentalized biography as the literary genre in which to expose the corruption undergirding local politics in Providence? What form of literary support did ordinary white women Rhode Islanders lend to *Memoirs of Elleanor Eldridge*?

Hundreds of biographies were published in the United States from 1790 through the end of the nineteenth century to perform the cultural work of shaping a (primarily hegemonic) national character. Miriam Elizabeth Burstein's explorations of the Huntington Library collections reveal that while academic women's studies in the 1980s stormed against an absence of women in the historical record, those second-wave feminists inspired—and in most cases, completed—the twenty-first century historiographical research that has exposed the lie of allegedly missing life stories. Burstein posits that in recent years "the attention [paid] to the historiography of women's history," including women's life histories, illustrates that "women had been finding historians for quite some time—centuries, in fact—and with the advent of cheap printing techniques, they [found] a great many more."[112] Among the leading early nineteenth-century US women's biographies were Lydia Maria Child's books *Good Wives* (1833), expanded and renamed in its fifth edition as *Biographies of Good Wives* (1846), and later reprinted under the title *Celebrated Women: or, Biographies of Good Wives* (1858). Meanwhile, Elizabeth Fries Ellet's nationalistic collections of portraits—chiefly, the acclaimed *The Women of the American Revolution* (1848)—depicted white women as heroes who sewed, cleaned, and prayed in service to the early republic.[113] In addition, according to Edith B. Gelles, white women's biography in early nineteenth-century New England included the "pious memoir": a short autobiographical account of religious conversion, usually a private chronicle not intended for public reading, that often formed the basis for textual commemorations of a deceased woman's life, that is, her obituary, as well as forming posthumous moral and religious instruction to younger people she left behind.[114]

Early obituaries of people of color have been established by Lois Brown as providing heretofore-overlooked access to early black life in colonial America.[115] Those aside, very few accounts of black (women's) lives were written and printed, due to prevailing questions about who merited attention as the subject of a biography: usually founding statesmen, military heroes, and other celebrities. Arguably, *Memoirs of Elleanor Eldridge* and *Elleanor's Second Book* form protofeminist biographies in that they challenge normative maleness as singularly suitable for the reconstruction of a life. Moreover, the biographies represent Eldridge's life as patriotic, humble, and self-sacrificing—subverting the centering of black subjects in religious and criminal confessions.

The first chapter of *Memoirs of Elleanor Eldridge* consists fully of endorsements. The first statement attesting to Eldridge's industry and nobility is signed by A.G.D. and dated July 19, 1838. A list of eleven women who have variously employed Eldridge then declares her to be ever "honest and faithful."[116] In addition, a Mrs. Nancy Webb verifies Eldridge's industry with a statement dated July 20, 1838. Eight days later, Mary B. Annable also testifies to Eldridge's prudence and respectability.[117] An appendix of eight poems, tributes, and other commendations at the end of the 1838 *Memoirs* further attests to white women's involvement in Eldridge and Whipple's enterprise. The first of these is an unsigned piece of prose titled "Appeal to Strangers, In behalf of the subject of the Narrative contained in this book";[118] it is narrated in the first-person singular. Following this appeal are endorsements from seven additional women; five of these testimonials are signed by M.W.; E.C.J.; "a Lady of Providence," who adds S.P. as her initials; C[atharine] R[ead] Williams (ca.1790–1872); M.A.; and finally F[rances] H[arriet] W[hipple], respectively. The narrator remarks that the second endorsement, by M.W., is "a piece written by a little girl. It brings to notice one trait of Ellen's character, that of unwearying kindness to children, which never fails to win their innocent little hearts, and fill them with the warmest love."[119] In an editor's note, Whipple further identifies the child-author as "my kind little cousin."[120] "The African's Appeal," signed by E.C.J., is an eighteen-line, first person plural, putatively African lament of black captivity.[121] The succeeding poem, "Hard Fate of Poor Ellen, by a Lady of Providence," whose author adds S.P. as her initials, also appeared in the December 7, 1838, issue of Garrison's *Liberator.*[122] S.P.'s first-person narrator pathetically describes her encounter with "Poor colored Ellen!"[123] Moving, but less maudlin, is "To the Public, In Behalf of Ellen," which is a prose tribute to Eldridge by Catharine Read Williams, a descendant of Rhode Island's prominent and influential Arnold patrilineage.[124] Williams's prose support is dated at Providence on October 19, 1838.[125] Following Williams's commendation, M.A.'s "To Ellen" strategically concludes with the opening lines of Thomas Moore's 1816 *Sacred Song* hymn "This World Is All a Fleeting Show."[126]

The final two works in the appendix, "The Supplication of Elleanor" and "The Emancipated," are signed with Whipple's initials, "F. H. W."[127] The penultimate of these long, last poems is dated November 7, 1838; thus, several documents in *Memoirs*'s appendix insinuate that that the biography was written between July and November 1838. "The Supplication of Elleanor" uses a first-person speaker analogue for Eldridge, as apparent in its account of an exoticized African "grandsire," a Narragansett mother, and a father who responded valiantly to national conscription "though the heavy chain had bent his body to the ground."[128] This poetic narrative of Eldridge's story in her own voice is ironic, for Whipple rarely inscribes that voice in the biography proper. However, as both concluding poems have "Elleanor" speak in the so-called Standard English of her day, Whipple uses them in conventional ways for progressive ends. As Gellman observes, "Sentimental poetry placed in the mouths of African speakers contradicted anecdotes that played off of alleged black ignorance and supposed faulty dialect."[129]

The proper names and initials used to signify Eldridge's supporters indicate at least eighteen different Rhode Island (white) women invested in aiding the African indigenous woman in the sale of her book and the recovery of her real estate property. These women probably owned little property themselves, for as Loren Schweninger found in a study of antebellum southern black women who owned property, "free black women controlled a substantially larger share of the black wealth than white women controlled of the white wealth."[130] Such was the case across the country during the antebellum era in the United States. Eldridge's ability to align herself with a stable and respected group of white women recalls Phillis Wheatley's savvy negotiation of the sociopolitical economy that would determine the sale of her book *Poems on Various Subjects.* As Joanna Brooks demonstrates in "Our Phillis, Ourselves," Wheatley sought a unique opportunity during the final weeks of her manuscript preparations to secure the signatures of "most of the prominent male citizens of Boston" when they gathered for a freeholders meeting "at Faneuil Hall on October 28, 1772."[131] Brooks cogently speculates that the poet used this occasion to circulate (herself or by proxy) a prepared statement affirming her talent; the signatures of eighteen "most respectable Characters in Boston"[132] thus endorsed Wheatley's capacity to write the poems she had penned. More significantly yet, Brooks "propose[s] one alternative narrative for understanding how she [Wheatley] made her groundbreaking career: not by securing a single endorsement by powerful men, but by cultivating an intricate network of relationships among white women. She [Wheatley] used elegies that mobilized her own grief and utilized her own canny understanding of the inner lives of white women to build a network of white female supporters; white women, for their part, used Wheatley to perform the emotional labor of condolence and sympathy for them."[133] Likewise, Eldridge used her relationships with white women respected in their local milieu as her principal resource for selling her life story and regaining the property she had purchased with her savings.

Whipple and Eldridge would have valued the material book form of Eldridge's life and recognized the subversive properties not only of the production and consumption of books but also of the generation of print (culture), especially by people of color—long before Frederick Douglass did a double take when he overheard his master suggest that an *ell,* or *L,* separated men from slaves.[134] As Gundaker infers, people of color in early nineteenth-century United States perceived that "the visual uniformity of print" afforded them "a kind of provisional visual equality."[135] Moreover, print enabled "the recording [of] ideas and opinions and provid[ed] means for black voices to enter segregated spaces."[136] Eldridge might also have valued her book as providing "a new experience for many white readers": the absorption of her life within their familiar (and familial) environments, yet at a convenient remove since the book did not require them to confront her actual physical presence.[137] However, as Gundaker notes, "Triumphant appropriations of print recurred with each poem, oration, sermon, and narrative [by a black person] printed."[138] Joanna Brooks, Frances Smith Foster, Eric Gardner, and other scholars have demonstrated that people of African descent in colonial New England developed print materials in each of these genres both independently and in collaboration with whites.[139] Moreover, they developed the means to work with diverse media: single-page broadsides, unbound pamphlets, freestanding posters, newspapers, and journals. *Memoirs of Elleanor Eldridge* contributed notably to this early black print culture, while its interracial, collaborative authorship simultaneously complicated that culture.

Albro's 1830s and 40s editions of *Memoirs of Elleanor Eldridge* are all comprised of 128 pages that measure 5.5 inches by 7.38 inches. Each ran considerably longer than the average biography printed in a volume of similar dimensions. For example, the 1834 edition of Benjamin B. Thatcher's biography of Phillis Wheatley runs thirty-six pages. In contrast, the *Biography of Mrs. Semantha Mettler, the Clairvoyant,* which Whipple (Green) published some twelve years after the 1847 edition of *Memoirs of Elleanor Eldridge,* exceeds the length of Eldridge's biography only by 10 pages; the physical measurements of the two bound volumes are the same. In terms of slave narratives contemporaneous with the first *Memoirs of Elleanor Eldridge, The History of Mary Prince* originally consisted of forty pages and Pringle's foreword of two more pages. The third and last edition of David Walker's *Appeal to the Colored Citizens of the World,* the incendiary political tract of 1830, consists of eighty-eight pages. In other words, genre and year or era do not appear to have determined or influenced the length of a text documenting the lives of black people in the first half of the nineteenth century.

Among the various traditions and genres that *Memoirs* engaged and advanced is the domestic arts manual. Scholars have identified *The House Servant's Directory* (1827), a 180-page bound book by South Carolina-born Robert Roberts (1775–1860) as "the first commercially published book by an African American."[140] While Roberts's *Directory* was perhaps the first commercial bound book ostensibly unrelated to slavery and antislavery activism, it followed by three years the autobiography *Life of William Grimes, the Runaway Slave*, published in 1824.[141] *The House Servant's Directory* offered instruction in manners, cuisine, and domestic arts; it was written while Roberts served Christopher Gore, a former Massachusetts governor and senator in Waltham, Massachusetts.[142] Roberts's *Directory* was published in 1827, 1828, 1843, 1969, 1993, 1998, and 2006.

Neither Roberts's *Directory* nor *Memoirs of Elleanor Eldridge* emerged from the radical circumstances that yielded some black books such as Walker's *Appeal*. Given that early bound books were published by individuals or small groups, formal and informal, capable of investing financially in a print enterprise, it is no surprise that publishers sponsoring African American print texts in the late eighteenth and early nineteenth centuries were frequently members of Prince Hall Masons and other African American institutions of literacy, including lyceums, reading societies, church groups, black school boards, and benevolent societies. Such structures, as Foster asserts, worked to "create and preserve consensus and ideals, to record and report deeds and intentions, duties, rituals, routines and declarations" to build positive identities for people of African descent.[143] In some cases, African American churches started their own publishing companies to edit, print, and distribute documents, and moreover, founded schools to promote and develop literacy.[144] Many African Americans joined forces to "reclaim and rearticulate their political subjectivity in a space ungoverned by whites," as Brooks cogently contends in "The Early American Public Sphere and the Emergence of a Black Print Counterpublic."[145] From those alliances, black print culture grew out of early African American agitation against "unequal economic property relations proceeding from the historical institution of slavery and its legal abolition in the early national north."[146] As Brooks asserts, "The birth of black institutions and black print production in the 1780s and 1790s constitutes a crucial moment in the history of black thought about the public sphere, when black people articulate in practice and enact for the first time *in print* key principles of black counter-publicity: collective incorporation, conscious differentiation, and criticism of dominant political and economic interests."[147] Such were not the social or economic circumstances that culminated in such bound commodities as Wheatley's *Poems on Various Subjects* (1773), Roberts's *Directory*, or Eldridge's biographies, all of which relied instead on blacks' cunning engagement of white networks to secure publication of their black thought.[148]

Unlike colonial publishers, early nineteenth-century commercial printers did not necessarily proclaim any particular ideological investment in what they produced. Indeed, Benjamin T. Albro (1812–1873), who printed *Memoirs of Elleanor Eldridge*, served a clientele representing a relatively wide variety of interests but with service to counterhegemonic enterprises sufficient to command Whipple's respect. Through his printing company in Millsbury, Massachusetts, in July 1832 Albro published *The Millbury Patriot and Worcester County Workingmen's Advocate*, a labor newspaper begun one year earlier as *The Plebian, and Millbury Workingmen's Advocate*.[149] Before printing the first edition of *Memoirs*, Albro's offices had been "located on Elmwood Street" in Millbury, Rhode Island. In 1838, when Whipple hired the firm to print *Memoirs*, the B. T. Albro Printing Office had moved to No. 78 North Main Street in downtown Providence, Rhode Island. An 1840 receipt specifies the range of services provided by the office as follows: "Books, Pamphlets, Circulars, Cards, Invoices, Bills of Lading, Manufacturers Tickets from Xylographic Plates, Bank Checks, Blank Bills, Handbils [sic], Shop Bills, and any other description of Printing that may be required, will be executed in good styles, and at low prices. Ink of various colors always at hand, for fancy work."[150] By 1843, Albro had moved to 2 Canal Street in Providence and was still printing editions of both *Memoirs of Elleanor Eldridge* and *Elleanor's Second Book*; he continued to print annual editions of one or both biographies for the next several years. In addition, Albro published funeral sermons, including *The Virtuous Woman Commended. A Sermon, Preached in Franklin. May 3, 1840. Occasioned by the Death of Mrs. Hannah Miller, Wife of*

Nathaniel Miller, M.D., by Jacob Ide, D. D.; temperance tracts such as the *Cold Water Magazine* for the Temperance Reformation in Providence as late as June 1843 or perhaps longer;[151] both anti- and pro-capital punishment pamphlets; sheet music; working people's news; and local news. He also printed *A Statement of the Case of the First General Baptist Church in Warwick, R. I. with Elder Henry Tatem* in 1838.

Thus, it is not surprising that Whipple hired Albro to print *Memoirs of Elleanor Eldridge,* as his various printing jobs correlate with her clear authorial and activist devotion to working-class Americans and especially to New England's working poor. Moreover, Albro's office issued "the first number of the Dorrite paper, the New Age and Constitutional Advocate," which would have won Whipple over.[152] In other words, Albro might have influenced themes Whipple would later address, and Whipple seems to have chosen him as her local printer because she was already writing about topics his other printed materials engaged— topics ranging, along with those noted above, from Presbyterian religious confessions, temperance tracts, local and state histories, and society catalogs.[153] Later Whipple (as Frances H. Green) would publish *Analytical Class-book of Botany, Designed for Academics and Private Students.*[154]

Memoirs of Elleanor Eldridge and *Productions of Maria W. Stewart*

What knowledge emerges if, in search of authoritative historiographies of workers' struggles and entrepreneurial efforts by African American women and other women of color, we apply social historians' tools of weaving together a fabric from swatches and remnants of individual women's stories? Although 19th-century official state documents omitted more than they recorded, can we not locate in their disparate stories (black and indigenous) women's unflagging devotion to seize and protect their rights to income as well as to the social and financial independence and the property they purchased with capital justly gained?

A measure of the politics of publishing *Memoirs of Elleanor Eldridge* appears through contrasting Eldridge with Maria W. Stewart (b. 1803), the African American orator who—as Eldridge and Whipple were collaboratively writing Eldridge's biography—left Boston (approximately fifty-two miles northeast of Providence) after a career of courageous and revolutionary violations of social codes rigidly enforced by both whites and people of color. Stewart was one of the first women in the United States to address public audiences of both men and women and audiences representing different racial categories, and she did so in the radical public space of Boston's African Meeting House. After being orphaned at age five in 1808 (as Eldridge was considered to have been after the death of her mother) Stewart was indentured until age fifteen; for her service she received rudimentary book learning, which she afterward enriched through attendance at Boston's Sabbath schools for blacks.[155] Like Eldridge, Stewart developed skill in homemaking arts and, for a time, earned her living through domestic service.[156] Later, however, her speeches would call for a radical revision of black women's labors, appealing to women for social activism to raise their moral, educational, and fiscal standards and aspirations.

Stewart's speeches also specifically called for black men's support of women's intellectual and professional development beyond the domestic service economy. She found a mentor in David Walker, author of the masculinist and nationalist *Appeal to the Colored Citizens of the World* (1829).[157] Walker died prematurely in 1830. Only months before, on December 17, 1829, Stewart's husband, entrepreneur, and ship's outfitter James W. Stewart, had died after they had been married a mere three years. With James, Maria Stewart had lived in Boston's free black community, which Marilyn Richardson describes as comprised of "waiters, coachmen, sailors, barbers and hairdressers, dealers in new and used clothing, tailors, wood sawyers, musicians, and teamsters, among other jobs."[158] As a widow, Stewart launched an extraordinarily public career as a political writer and speaker.

Stewart's first public articulations of unorthodox gender views were published in 1831 as the pamphlet *Religion and the Pure Principles of Morality, the Sure Foundation on Which We Must Build,*[159] which Katherine Clay Bassard assesses as "her most sustained political and theological analysis."[160] Addressing Boston's Afro-Protestant community, Stewart turned to biblical and religious precepts to argue for radical social and political activism; she invoked the spiritual and social values of fledgling Afro-Protestantism, including its focus on the integrity of the "respectable," middle-class, heteronormative, male-dominated black family. Even as she admonished, "Let each one strive to excel in good housewifery, knowing that prudence and economy are the road to wealth," Stewart more vociferously questioned, in the pages of *Religion and the Pure Principles*, "How long shall the fair daughters of Africa be compelled to bury their minds and talents beneath a load of iron pots and kettles? Until union, *knowledge* and love begin to flow among us" (italics added).[161] In other words, she preached black republican motherhood, and called both for black women's cultivation of domestic arts within their homes and for their commitment to excelling within the politico-economic sphere. Challenging the white supremacist and chauvinist politics that had deprived Eldridge of access to formal education, Stewart advocated for black women's scholastic development and their active participation in public life. Within a few years, her radical orations had provoked her audiences such that she felt forced to leave Boston. In her "Farewell Address," delivered in Boston on September 21, 1833, she grieved the hostile reception she had received from her African American neighbors, saying, "I am about to leave you, perhaps, never more to return. For I find it is no use for me as an individual to try to make myself useful among my color in this city."[162] As Stewart departed Boston, Eldridge and Whipple were joining forces to produce *Memoirs of Elleanor Eldridge*, the aim of which, too, was an exposé and an end to broad patriarchal power; they specifically targeted white men, since the latter had seized Eldridge's property.

Before Eldridge's land rights cases began in 1835, Stewart had unsuccessfully sued at court in 1829 for her deceased husband's pension for service in the War of 1812. Stewart's biographer, Richardson, describes the "legal maneuvers" deployed for over two years by corrupt white businessmen determined to profit from James W. Stewart's death as "so blatant and shameless that even the presiding judge found them hard to stomach"—not unlike the trials the widow suffered on the lecture platform in Boston.[163] By entering the public sphere, Stewart had bravely exposed herself to greater "insults and indignities, unlike anything experienced by [her] white brothers and sisters."[164] Thus the audiences Stewart faced validated Eileen Boris's surefooted contention that "work itself creates gender" and that "bodies stand as both physical and symbolic sites . . . as a central arena for the playing out of racial-ized gender in class society."[165] Decades after she delivered her "Farewell Address," Stewart finally won her widow's pension in a second suit after the Civil War.

Eldridge's own economic success, one might say, was developed pre-cisely through means opposed by Stewart, and yet, ironically, Stewart possessed a higher social status than did Eldridge, a ranking akin to a greater class status but without the attendant actual wealth. While both women were financially victimized by white men and lived in cities with close proximity to one another in the same years, Eldridge and Stewart had two very different publishing experiences because one was literate and had stronger ties to literate men. Stewart's literacy and location in Boston gave her access to different kinds of black com-munities, including her ties to black nationalist David Walker and to the abolitionist William Lloyd Garrison, who published many of her writings in his *Liberator*. Significantly, Stewart lacked male benefac-tors, and this absence, as Ebony Utley notes, "removed all practical prohibitions from her entrance to the public sphere."[166] As a widow, her own educational and speaking opportunities enabled her to sus-tain herself as an abolitionist, orator, and writer. Ironically, Stewart's speeches called blacks to the cultivation more of western "civiliza-tion" and white bourgeois sociopolitical pursuits than the mainte-nance of African cultural conventions or practices infused with syn-cretic Anglo-Africanisms.[167] In this way, she fostered codes of conduct among Boston's black middle class. Her speeches argued passionately that women, no less than men, were able to lead black movements for political and civil rights. Yet, notwithstanding the protofeminist ardor of her speeches, Stewart would identify herself as *Mrs. Stewart* in the title *Productions*, perhaps to curry cultural, moral, and social capital where she lacked actual monetary resources.[168] Conversely, Eldridge seems to have studiously avoided marriage despite whatever social gains the title "Mrs." might have effected for her; from the frontis-piece to the final poems in any edition of *Memoirs of Elleanor Eldridge*, Eldridge appears first and foremost as a worker rather than a lady or an intellectual—not so much shunning Stewart's tacit politics of respectability as fiscally succeeding in spite of it.[169] Ultimately, if property values are the measure, then Eldridge's fiscal achievements confirm *she* was actually more upwardly mobile than Stewart, rendering hers a complex class status in light of *Memoirs*'s apparent disregard for a collective advancement of women of color and its failure to protest against systemic economic discrimination subjugating African Americans and indigenous peoples in the workforce.

A Free Woman of Property

And Malawi saw . . . a vessel a hundred times the size of the thatch-roofed homes in his village. . . . This he heard the phantoms call the Providence.

—Charles Johnson[170]

In the beginning black autobiography conceived of life as a difficult journey toward some sort of ultimate blessedness.

—William L. Andrews[171]

As we construct and interpret the facts of a narrative, we are also creating another narrative; we are making history.

—Frances Smith Foster[172]

What were Elleanor Eldridge's ancestral origins such that she matured into adulthood sufficiently affluent to purchase considerable real estate property, even to owning more than any other woman of color in Providence and the surrounding area? Was hers inherited wealth—or that earned through her own labors? Did Rhode Island's socioeconomic contexts construct a class hierarchy that included a space for self-made women of color as early as 1830? Could a working woman (of color) fit neatly into New England's early republic black elite? What exactly constituted upper-class-ness, "the better sort," among blacks in Eldridge's day anyway?[173] How does the frontispiece portrait of Eldridge in *Memoirs of Elleanor Eldridge* work to reconcile the paradoxes of her social identities as a free black and wealthy working woman?

According to *Memoirs*, the parents of Elleanor Eldridge's father, Robin Eldridge, were captured in Zaire and forced through the Middle Passage, and her mother, *née* Hannah Prophet, descended from the regionally renowned Narragansett elder Chloe Prophet. Thus, Elleanor was born on March 26, 1785, into a Warwick, Rhode Island, family of bound men of African descent and an indigenous matrilineage multiple generations free.[174] (Providence *Births, Marriages, and Deaths* records list Eldridge's death date as June 24, 1862.[175]) She was fortunate not only in having been born precisely one year into Rhode Island emancipation but also into a city that "in particular sought to prevent the establishment of hereditary African slavery in the colony."[176] *Memoirs* identifies Eldridge's maternal grandmother as Mary Fuller (1678–1780), "a native Indian" of the Fuller clan and "probably a portion of the Narragansett tribe . . . who witnessed the departing glories of her tribe."[177] Enslaved persons of indigenous, African, or multiracial ancestry were often referenced simply as *slave* in eighteenth century colonial documents; nonetheless, Whipple's use of *slave* to characterize Thomas Prophet, Mary's spouse purchased (and presumably freed) from white slaveholders, seems Whipple's sign that Thomas was of African descent and thus, their daughter Hannah, Elleanor's mother, of biracial heritage.[178]

Rhode Island's first census was collected in 1790; it documents 427 free blacks (or rather, free "blacks" since state officials had by then begun to eclipse and collapse ethnic and ancestral lines otherwise distinguishing one group of people of color from another), but Eldridge's kin are not among them.[179] *Memoirs* reports that her father Robin [variously named Robert] Eldridge was forcibly brought from western Africa to Rhode Island with his parents and siblings. According to *Memoirs*, Eldridge's parents married before her father's service in the American Revolution. Robin Eldridge and Hannah Prophet produced nine children together, five of whom lived to adulthood; Elleanor was born "the last of seven successive daughters."[180] Eldridge was a small child when Hannah died and not yet twenty when her father died.

The Baker family, for whom Hannah periodically worked as a Warwick washerwoman, had a daughter named Elleanor; this child had urged her own name for that of Hannah's infant daughter, and thereafter, the *Memoirs* states, Elleanor Baker "always continued to take great interest in her little colored name-sake."[181] "Not long after" Hannah's death, Elleanor Baker sought Robin Eldridge's permission to indenture his daughter, her namesake, in part because New England custom regarded a motherless child as an orphan; he consented, the story goes, "with this remark, that she would not stay a week."[182] However, shrewd and obviously already insightful about raced power negotiations, in all likelihood aware of the white supremacist discrimination against her parents as individual people of color and as an interracial married couple (notwithstanding Rhode Island's reductive encoding of Hannah as categorically black or "colored"), prepubescent Elleanor agreed to serve the family for one year and "fixed her price at 25 cents per week."[183] More typically at the turn into the nineteenth century in New England, "local officials routinely placed minor children under guardianship when their fathers died."[184] After 1800, orphaned children of color, like their white counterparts, were dependent for their welfare on "officials [who] contracted with a man who would act as a proper father" until the children became adults, which for girls was usually designated as age eighteen, and in Rhode Island in particular, girls and young women of color performed contractual labor through age twenty-one.[185] Indeed, as David Silverman reports, "over the course of the eighteenth and early nineteenth centuries nearly all Indians in southern New England were affected in some way by indentured servitude."[186] Indentured service could run for twelve years or more.[187]

Eldridge seems not to have been taught to read or write in childhood. Although indentured servitude in colonial Rhode Island provided some indigenous children with rudimentary education, John E. Murray and Ruth Wallis Herndon report that "before 1798 [in Rhode Island], masters were under no obligation to educate pauper apprentices."[188] While "about a quarter of all Rhode Island children [apprentices] were promised further education," the state "had no legal requirements to educate children until 1798."[189] Moreover, as Gundaker explains, "free and enslaved people grasped, and actively created, opportunities to read and write," but Eldridge seems never to have pursued book learning.[190] She was thirty-six years old in 1821 when the African Union Meeting House opened a school for children of color in Providence. However, her many domestic skills and her business success document her exceptional innate intelligence, including her talent for creating and seizing personal opportunities.

After her indenture with the Bakers, Eldridge served as a spinner to the family of a Captain Benjamin Greene at Warwick Neck, Rhode Island.[191] Apparently working for the Greene family in a craft apprenticeship that provided training in housewifery (through spinning, laundering, painting, wallpapering, and the like), Eldridge developed the skills that she would apply to her entrepreneurship as an independent adult.[192] From 1801 to 1809, from ages sixteen to twenty-four, Eldridge learned dairying, the foundation of her later expertise in cheese making. Also, at some point, she gained the ability and experience to become an exceptional weaver. Weaving required considerable skill in preindustrial eras. The *Memoirs*'s references to Eldridge's ability to find paid work as a weaver (and later, a house painter and wallpaperer) elucidate how she could earn the capital to lift her into the ranks of property owners. Moreover, the significant demand of expert handloom weaving for families made her a very desirable person for households to hire for periods of time to create the fabric that would then be cut and sewn by a seamstress. During this transitional time in the production of woven cloth, before it was fully mechanized, Eldridge's abilities and talents handily aligned with real US household needs.[193]

In 1804, Eldridge traveled on foot from Providence to Adams, Massachusetts, to help one of her sisters attend to the business of their deceased father's estate in Warwick, Rhode Island, where Eldridge and her siblings were born. The estate business required "some legal advices from a daughter, then residing in the north-western part of Massachusetts." *Memoirs* skirts the matter of literacy needed to finalize the estate by asserting that the "difficulties attending a communication by mail" were greater then than at present. But the biography affirms Eldridge's filial and familial loyalty by noting that Ellen volunteered to make the journey, and attend to the business.[194] In this way Eldridge's commitment to both kin and clan emerges in such accounts of devotion to other people of color.

Eldridge mastered several additional profitable trades that she turned into a successful profession. These skills placed her in a rare social and financial situation: she maintained a lucrative business whereas the majority of employment positions available to free(d) black women in and near Providence were restricted to the domestic labors they had performed before Rhode Island enacted emancipation.[195] A few fortunate free black women in antebellum New England, Eldridge among them, cultivated and traded such skills in the domestic arts as quilting, sewing, and cheese-making; they were generally involved in such trades and businesses as dressmaking, school-teaching, import-export mercantilism, hat-making and millinery shop-keeping, running boarding houses or taking in boarders, and hairdressing or keeping hair salons.[196]

Did Eldridge's greater wealth and entrepreneurial authority propel her into a more elite socioeconomic class than other women (of African descent) who worked with their hands but not for themselves? To answer this question, Melish contends that we need "to revisit the question of exactly who the antebellum 'working class' was, a question made more urgent by recent attempts to reconsider the utility of class as an explanatory category and to reshape its definition."[197] The complications of defining socioeconomic class in the early national United States are addressed by David Roediger, whose book *The Wages of Whiteness* demonstrates that middle-class status for antebellum people of African descent was determined by labor: skill determined access to wealth. Locating Eldridge's class status requires understanding class as a fluid, unstable, and often contradictory category of analysis, in which capitalism intersects with citizenship and civil rights.[198] The precarious state of human and civil rights for people of color in antebellum Rhode Island limited the extent to which they could pursue property. They faced, as Frances Smith Foster and Claudia May observe, a doubly binding bootstraps myth that claimed economic class advancement could be determined and controlled by individual effort, fortitude, and merit. In truth, however, class aspirations were and remain insufficient to situate a (black) person in a particular socioeconomic class. As illustrated in the discussion above of Eldridge's class privileges and limitations in contradistinction to Maria Stewart's, class location for people of African descent in 1830s New England depended on interlocking systems of power, that is, at the intersections of such constructions as heritage and ancestry, education and literacy, and religious affiliation (namely the Christian denomination). However, as Leonard Curry warns, "'the very few practitioners of entrepreneurial occupations [including Eldridge] had, if anything, even less likelihood of achieving any significant degree of economic success'" than did the rare persons of color represented in the professional class including clerks, school teachers, and ministers.[199]

In any case, *Memoirs* situates Eldridge "among her people, in the very highest niche of aristocracy" after her brother George was elected to governor, a class location presumably sustained when George Eldridge was reelected thrice more.[200] Eldridge's access to capital, too, illustrates the contrast between her greater wealth (if not a commensurate economic class status) and Stewart's. Eldridge is said to have traveled discreetly "with the good substantial sum of sixty dollars," for example, when she crossed two states to settle her father's estate.[201] In other words, while Eldridge's status as a free woman possessing desired domestic skills and an astute business sense with which to market them gave her the financial means to acquire considerable property, debt free, the acquisition of her wealth through physical rather than intellectual labors, however professionalized, limited her social standing as a black leader, and her female gender identity further curtailed the reach of her political power to influence social or public policy. If an African American "middle class" is defined as a group made up of persons of African descent who "sought and supported 'racial uplift' or 'race pride' through education, employment, and political empowerment,"[202] the verbal portrait of Eldridge that emerges in *Memoirs of Elleanor Eldridge* situates her outside the black middle class of her day.

A visual frontispiece portrait of Eldridge prefaces each edition of *Memoirs of Elleanor Eldridge*; reading it from different angles illuminates the complexity of her socioeconomic class location. Arguably, the extent to which Eldridge is known at all correlates to awareness of this portrait, revolutionary in that it forms one of a very few extant positive, "fully realized," respectful images of early nineteenth-century women of color. For Eldridge came of age just after the South African Sarah Baartman, staged in Paris as the freakish Hottentot Venus, and other black and indigenous women the world over were viciously mocked, caricatured, and lampooned as a matter of course, to exalt (and contain) European womanhood.[203] Augusta Rohrbach calculates that "Six out of ten slave narratives published in the United States between 1845 and 1870 provided a portrait of the author as a frontispiece," presumably to validate both the actual existence of their black subjects and their alleged African ancestry.[204] Indeed, Michael A. Chaney has characterized author portraits in slave narratives so essential as to be "*de rigueur*."[205] Eldridge's portrait follows the inclusion of images of black subjects in slave narratives as well as, ironically, the tradition of author portraits such as the frontispiece to Wheatley's *Poems on Various Subjects*, from which it differs so dramatically in that Eldridge was not conventionally schooled.[206] Eldridge's portrait has been reproduced across academic disciplines, in, for example, Sterling's *We Are Your Sisters*, Xiomara Santamarina's *Belabored Professions: Narratives of African American Working Womanhood*, and Rohrbach's *Truth Stranger than Fiction: Race, Realism, and the U.S. Literary Marketplace*.[207] The prominence—indeed, celebrity—of Eldridge's portrait derives partly from its representation of creditable, respectable black womanhood and black female class prestige.

Importantly, too, the portrait not only signals Eldridge's self-determination, but it also signals her resolve to show herself an agent—in spite of her need for authorial collaboration to publish her story. One of the advantages of including a frontispiece is that it underscores Eldridge's ways of knowing other than conventional academic schooling, which she seems not to have received. Participating in the arrangement and production of the frontispiece to her biography, Eldridge could exert power over her portrait without being proficient as a reader or writer of English because such images speak to those who both are and are not formally trained to read books. In that images of women of African descent can be "read" as a language, a matter of linguistics, with the inclusion of the frontispiece portrait, Eldridge literally and figuratively invested in the publication of her life story. For notwithstanding significant differences between the arts of painting and photography, we might nonetheless apply to Eldridge's portrait Alan Trachtenberg's notion of the literariness of photography, its linguistics practices involving realism and truth telling.[208] Trachtenberg further notes the necessary collaborations between photographers and their sitters.[209] Drawing from that notion, we can conceptualize the frontispiece to

Memoirs of Elleanor Eldridge as attesting as well to a negotiation, a carefully managed collaboration between Eldridge as portrait sitter, the artist who drew her image, perhaps Whipple also, and certainly Albro in his role as printer. As the artistic subject, Eldridge collaborated on the orchestration of an autobiographical portrait to the extent that she worked with the artist, the printer, and perhaps her interlocutor, too, to represent herself as a complex social figure depicting several interlocking identities, none threatening and all pleasing to white and other readers who would purchase her biography, perhaps particularly because the image represented her as trustworthy and desirable to employ. Mutual responsibility for the final product lay in all parties' arrangement of the sitter's body, of light and shadow, backdrop, furniture, the positions of the sitter's limbs and gaze, what clothing she wore, how positioned, and so on: as in photographic portraits after 1839, so, too, in Eldridge's frontispiece portrait of 1838. Ultimately, then, Eldridge exerted a measure of power over the image of her that preceded the narrative of her life.

The portrait figures Eldridge as a woman of African descent and we can read it also as a figure of indigenous descent. One of the most notable details of Eldridge's portrait is the direct and confident gaze with a slight smile and exposed hair; significantly, the figure in the image returns the gaze of the artist and the spectator. The person of color depicted has a direct gaze that conveys moral self-assurance, not subjugation or defiance as some white spectators would have been socialized to expect in an image of a black or indigenous person, based on caricatures, stereotypes, and cartoons in broadsides.[210] The small size of the population of African Americans and indigenous peoples remaining in Rhode Island by Eldridge's adulthood would have made it unlikely for the average white person to encounter black people often in the course of a day, so the image might have been all that some white readers would know of nonwhites.[211] Moreover, "race" is depicted in this portrait through the representation of an "African" phenotype and curly "African" hair, not straight hair as figured in the stereotypical Native American "squaw." It is no coincidence that the figure appears alone, not only in keeping with traditional author frontispiece portraits, but also to accentuate the subject's conformity to the iconic myth of rugged American individualism and to stress that, as a person alone, she represents no threat to white patriarchy or white supremacy: she is not a member of a mutinous community of color, and she apparently has no *male* spouse and no dependent children. This encouraging aspect of her character is highlighted by the empty space of the background behind her: she is an isolated "colored" figure suspended in a vacuum—decontextualized, androgynous, tranquil, safe.[212]

The figure in the frontispiece to *Memoirs of Elleanor Eldridge* is gendered female in a variety of ways, each of which repudiates interlocking racist and sexist stereotypes of Mammy, wench, Sambo, squaw, indigenous warrior, and black insurrectionist. Eldridge is depicted wearing apparel covered by a woman's light-colored shawl modestly draped around her neck and broad shoulders (however, notably in a style not uncommon among Native American men and women). Although her work as a housepainter and wallpaper hanger might have been work done by both men and women, thus immasculating her to a degree, for the portrait she dresses in feminine garments, the trappings of respectable white womanhood, that conventional readers would understand, expect, and respect, with a shawl—but no apron or turban or bandana. The shawl in particular authenticates her female gender identity; the white shawl and its color offer visual proof of the verbal text's claims of Eldridge's modesty and chastity. In addition, the shawl reminds readers of her exceptional (rare) skill as a handloom weaver.

Eldridge was approximately fifty-three years old when the first edition of *Memoirs* was published in 1838. If the portrait is intended to represent her at that age, then she is illustrated as a robust, vigorous worker. The frontispiece portrays Eldridge as satisfied and capable, too, tacitly playing up ostensible advantages of depicting her having "manly" strength through its suggestions of her androgyny by foreshortening and exaggerating her right arm and foregrounding it, to lead the spectator's gaze directly to it. Still, the portrait also abnegates multiple challenges Eldridge likely faced in her actual work. That is, *Memoirs of Elleanor Eldridge* and *Elleanor's Second Book* deftly skirt every detail that could incline readers toward (mis)construing the subject as plaintive about her sociopolitical station or about ailments she suffered due to her employers' racism, sexism, xenophobia, or material or environmental neglect. Working in white homes entailed significant risks for women of color, ranging from physical and corporeal injury including a continuum of sexual assaults, to harmful working conditions, to various forms of sado-psychological injury. Moreover, they were routinely subject to economic inequity as they had little recourse when white clients denied or turned them out of promised lodging, or refused to honor wage agreements.[213] Rather than any symbol of displeasure, Eldridge is flourishing a sign of her trade, perhaps a wallpapering brush. Here only, if at all, she makes a subtle political statement by aligning herself with local artisans. For, in years before political parties evolved, one form of political expression and practice by early republic urban artisans included processions in which, as Jeffrey L. Pasley phrases it in *Beyond the Founders*, they used "producerist language" to assert their civic virtue.[214]

While editions of *Memoirs of Elleanor Eldridge* were slightly altered over time, to correct typographical errors, for example, and to update the introduction to the second edition of *Memoirs* in 1840 (after the publication of the first edition of *Elleanor's Second Book* in 1839), the original portrait, an intaglio woodcut engraving, remains the same. By the time the last known edition of *Memoirs* was published in 1847, the daguerreotype had been available for nearly ten years but it was prohibitively expensive in print publication, that is, as a genre for the production of frontispiece author portraits. As Louis Masur has explained, "to reach a wider audience, daguerreotype portraits had to be engraved for publication, because the halftone process, which mechanically transfers photographs to the printed page, did not exist until the end of the [nineteenth] century" (1421).[215] The consistent use of the frontispiece portrait in every edition of both *Memoirs* and *Elleanor's Second Book* further supports an esteem of painting and drawing and a related initial worry about photography that lingers, though manifested perhaps in different ways across time. That is, as Masur observes, "painting, more than any other art form, is treated as the premier visual expression of our [i.e., US] culture. The nineteenth-century critic John Ruskin considered painting the most 'trustworthy' index of a nation's greatness, and that chauvinist notion continues to undergird how we think of pictures, what is displayed in museums, and what scholars write about"—even though there is increasing critique of who has and controls "access to the tools of cultural production and reproduction . . . to questions of social status and power" (1415–16).

Within the biography's overall framework, the frontispiece to *Memoirs of Elleanor Eldridge* tacitly represents a number of ironies that abound regarding its subject. The life narrative that follows the portrait establishes Eldridge as one who could choose not only her clients, but also the particular labors she performed for them and the amount she charged for her services. First, the frontispiece portrait prefaces the story of a free wage earner and property owner of color, a single woman who controls her voluntary labors and, moreover, her entrepreneurship. Then, the verbal narrative confirms that it owes its existence to the financial assistance of persons who have sponsored the subject's entrepreneurship. It narrates the story of the rise and fall of that business, and it boldly solicits financial assistance from readers. In other words, Whipple and Eldridge and the unnamed portraitist argue for readers' purchase of *Memoirs*, and thus their rescue of Eldridge's real estate property, by championing a tautological narrative in which the eponymous subject proves herself worthy by conforming to dominant notions of (white) race, (non-indigenous) civilization, and (middle-) class belonging. What Michael Chaney has written about "a double-coded significance" materializing in frontispiece portraits of formerly enslaved narrators, holds true for Eldridge: "In essence, one is civilized and free because one bears recognizable evidence of civilization adhering to the standards of the dominant group."[216] Ironically, too, perhaps the reason both Eldridge biographies remain silent on issues of sexualized violence against (free) working women of color is that the books were endorsed and authenticated by her white women employers whose notions of female respectability and decorum enabled them more to castigate forms of masculinist legal and racialized violence than to condemn any degree of sexual coercion and domination.

—

In 1827, when Eldridge was forty-two years old, Robert Roberts published his book *The House Servant's Directory*.[217] Drawing for his *Directory* on his service to Nathan Appleton, the politically and socially active Boston aristocrat, Roberts explicitly targeted caterers and entrepreneurs as his readers, and the two editions of his *Directory* affirm its popularity. Whether Eldridge was among its admirers is uncertain, due both to the complexities of identifying her economic class status, as discussed previously, and to *Memoirs's* silence about her ability to read or any participation she might have had with reading clubs for Providence's colored communities. Though her real estate acquisition and access to capital did not depend on conventional book learning, she was likely familiar with Roberts's *Directory*, the final page of which, for example, details instructions for wallpaper hanging, a key service Eldridge offered her clients; this text quite possibly influenced Eldridge's approaches to her developing and maintaining her business. That Roberts represented Boston's active and ambitious free black community is clear: a property owner since 1822, he left domestic service for work as a stevedore after the publication of his book, and, according to biographer Graham Russell Gao Hodges, Roberts became an active Prince Hall Mason and abolitionist in Boston's black community movements and even led an anti-colonization meeting at the African School House in Boston on February 12, 1831.[218]

Although Boston and Providence were only one hundred miles apart, there were important differences in the lives of their respective black middle-class communities. On the one hand, the sociopolitical experiences of William J. Brown in Providence paralleled Roberts's in Boston, their similarities based on comparable (and proscribed) educational levels and organizational leadership opportunities for black men. On the other hand, whereas Roberts belonged to a substantial black middle-income community in Boston that included elite abolitionists, the black social and political activists' community in which Brown circulated was significantly smaller and seems not to have included Eldridge, even though Brown's and Eldridge's respective life stories name Chloe Prophet as a common Narragansett maternal ancestor. Tragically and ironically, both Brown and Eldridge were involved in land disputes with Providence whites.[219] Nonetheless, perhaps guided at midlife by Roberts's *Directory*, Eldridge "accumulated enough capital with her earnings to buy a small house in Warwick, which she rented out for forty dollars a year. . . . She [spent] the coldest part of each winter as a servant in a private home, hotel, or boarding house."[220] Eldridge's assertion of capitalist ingenuity and earned wealth, together with the respect she won from white women clients brought her the wrath of jealous white men and with it many civic, legal, and personal problems.

Memoirs of Elleanor Eldridge and the Rhode Island Court of Common Pleas

> I have known a poor man of colour, who laboured night and day, to acquire a little money, and having acquired it, he vested it in a small piece of land, and got him a house erected thereon, and having paid for the whole, he moved his family into it, where he was suffered to remain about nine months, when he was cheated out of his property by a white man, and driven out of door! And is this not the case generally?
>
> —David Walker[221]

> She was, in a single moment, by a single stroke of the hammar [sic], deprived of all fruits of the severe labor of years; and not only so, but actually thrown into debt for many small bills, for repairs and alterations on her houses, which she had the honor to discharge, against the advices [sic] of some of her friends; even after the property for which they had been incurred, had been so cruelly stripped away.
>
> —Elleanor's Second Book[222]

What can we glean from Rhode Island court records about Eldridge's losses and reacquisition of her real estate property across the 1830s? Does the account of Eldridge's shifting ownership and loss of property in Memoirs of Elleanor Eldridge match that in the historical record?[223] Given the quotidian occurrence of white pilfering of black and indigenous real estate throughout US history, and given whites' commonplace manipulation of the legal system to swindle people of color of all manner of property, what made Eldridge's court cases exceptional?

Two remarkable features emerge in the latter pages of Memoirs of Elleanor Eldridge. One is that the narrative of Eldridge's land ownership and dispossession in Memoirs of Elleanor Eldridge differs conspicuously from that which emerges in the incomplete historical record;

thus, what we can reasonably infer forms a perplexing *us versus them* version of Eldridge's legal troubles. Second is that where *Memoirs* is a her-version-versus-mine of Eldridge's life up to its account of the land debacles, abruptly the tone, plot, and arc of the biography change, and a collective voice rails against patriarchal dominance. That is, if the narrative voice of the first seventy-five or so pages betray Whipple's and Eldridge's competition for control over the story, from Chapter 8 forward they seem to speak in unison in and of the umbrage they take at the audacity of white patriarchy to subject Eldridge (read womankind) to a series of legal assaults utterly at whim. For the marvel of Eldridge's court cases is not that the state was consistently engaged with racist white businessmen in relentless pursuit of all of Eldridge's property, but rather the marvel is the very inconsistency of their pursuit *and* Eldridge's clear refusal to be deterred by intermittent perfidy.[224]

While *Memoirs* describes an unequivocally heinous and greedy patriarchy out to overtake Eldridge's property, the legal documents clarify that local businessmen sought to exploit Eldridge—and that these same men and sometimes others of their ilk would at other times negotiate fairly with her. No logic or pattern develops in their efforts alternately to steal her property or help her protect it. Likewise, the Providence Court of Common Pleas ruled against Eldridge in some of the cases in which she was named, and at other times on equivalent evidence they ruled in her favor. Court records substantiate some plaintiffs' claims that Eldridge defaulted on loans in her name, exposing her as one of many distressed borrowers with floundering resources in Rhode Island's volatile economy of the 1820s. *Memoirs*, too, now lambastes, now conceals charges that Eldridge intended to defraud her lenders, insisting rather on her victimhood by larcenous white men.

Ultimately, on one hand, taken together, what Rhode Island's extant legal records, *Memoirs of Elleanor Eldridge*, and *Elleanor's Second Book* reveal is that early national tyrannies were intersectional and systemic, but not systematic nor predictable; they were arbitrary and amorphous. On the other hand, what the discrepancies between the historical record and the Eldridge biographies illuminate is that although a "true story" of Eldridge's land disputes is inaccessible, the multiple reconstructions are all nonetheless useful, instructive, and poignant.

Both *Memoirs* and the available court records illuminate Eldridge's achievement of the now classic American dream of home ownership, which doubles for many as a material manifestation of the abstract notion of freedom. However, whereas Cameron B. Blevins posits that "a greater understanding of [Venture] Smith's real-estate records gives voice to their own fascinating narrative, one that *largely avoids the problematic issues of authorship* and authenticity surrounding his written narrative," the account of Eldridge's land woes in *Memoirs* juxtaposed against the extant court records documenting the legal cases centered on her land only confound attempts to understand any actual sequence of events.[225] Or, from another perspective, as Ruth Herndon and Ella Wilcox Sekatau assert, "We need both resources [native narratives and colonial documents] to reconstruct the relations between Narragansett people and Rhode Island leaders in the eighteenth century, and we find the oral history of the Narragansett people particularly important as a corrective to the archival sources."[226] *Memoirs* asserts that, in 1812, Eldridge left her work as spinner for the family of Captain Benjamin Greene in Warwick to join her sister Lettise and their younger siblings.[227] There, she began a "miscellaneous business" as a soap-maker, weaver, spinner, "nurse, washer, &c."[228] Three years later, *Memoirs* notes that she left Warwick to launch a business with another sister in Providence, adding to her services such skills as whitewashing and wallpapering.[229]

With income from these ventures, Eldridge began to purchase real estate property in Providence, and over time she built houses on the property for lease to tenants of color.[230] That she was financially able to make this purchase demonstrates Eldridge's extraordinary success in maintaining the trust of her white patrons in postemancipation Rhode Island's increasingly hostile climate toward people of color; without substantial work opportunities and the good will of moneyed clients, she could not have acquired her property. Notably, too, Eldridge's investment in real estate illustrates self-confidence, even valor, for *Memoirs of Elleanor Eldridge* testifies to her awareness of ways both her indigenous and her African parents and foreparents had been variously defrauded of their lands. US social historians have concluded that during the eighteenth century, "Indians also realized that any property they might accumulate was at risk of being appropriated by Englishmen who sued them for debt or charged them with personal injury," and moreover, powerful colonial whites obviously had (or seemed to have) far more support from white judges and jurors than African and Native Americans did, even the property owners among the latter.[231] Despite this menacing legacy, Providence court records include a deed dated May 18, 1826, issued from William E. Clarke to Eldridge and witnessed by then Town Clerk Nathan W. Jackson. A second affidavit also filed on May, 18, 1826, indicates an additional legal proceeding took place that day: this receipt documents a payment of $320 from Eldridge (a "Providence Single Woman of Colour") to Clarke, for the purchase of a 50-foot square lot in "westerly" Providence "between High Street and [?] Street," that is, the "westerly part of Lot No 55 . . . on the plat off the Nathan Angell Lot." Furthermore, the lot contained "a certain wooden Building [?] for a Dwelling House."[232] This deed additionally specifies legal rights Eldridge accrued with her purchase, including the rights to "lawfully, peaceably and quietly have, hold, use, occupy, possess and enjoy, the said demised and bargained Premises."[233] Through painful and criminal irony, these very rights would be challenged and over-turned in later years, as white statesmen and businessmen sporadically dispossessed her of her Providence real estate properties and aided her in regaining them in a veritable shuffleboard for gain and sport.

Among the circumstances rendering Eldridge vulnerable to patri-archal caprice was a regional typhus fever epidemic. Sometime in the early 1820s, she contracted a severe case of typhus fever.[234] After her lengthy convalescence from this illness, her growing business often required her to travel to other parts of New England, and frequently to accompany her employers—an aspect of her business that enabled her to demand higher wages than her competitors. Although Eldridge was a property owner, *Memoirs* reports that she sometimes lived with or near her employers, paying little rent, if any, while collecting her own leasing fees from her tenants. Her close proximity to her employers at least once included travel to Connecticut as a nurse accompanying one white woman employer whose daughter was sick. While *Memoirs* does not specify the date Eldridge first contracted typhus, it cites September 1831 as the month she suffered a second bout.[235] To recover a second time, she initially moved into the home of her brother George in Warwick, Rhode Island. With a measure of her health restored after six weeks, she persuaded him to accompany her to Adams, Massachusetts, for her recovery among women relatives.[236] *Memoirs* reports that Eldridge spent many months there.

Memoirs of Elleanor Eldridge cites spring 1832 as the season of Eldridge's return to Providence to find her rental properties confiscated—one of numerous legal entanglements Eldridge would face over time.[237] That date seems to contradict a promissory note dated February 20, 1834, which documents Eldridge's formal acknowledgment of a debt of $376 to George Carder of Warwick, Rhode Island; this promissory note also stipulates Eldridge's pledge to pay interest on the debt.[238] While the records do not specify her plans for the money she borrowed, that Eldridge spent the funds to acquire land is also unsurprising. According to Quigley and Finkelman, "In 1834 blacks in Providence owned $18,400 worth of real estate and $1,200 worth of personal property."[239] Eldridge was among these property holders of African descent. Notably here, too, in its collaboratively authored account of the events of spring 1832, the previously double-voiced *Memoirs* reverberates in a new univocal register.

A year later, two other available court records, both also witnessed by Sheriff Mann, allege that Eldridge defaulted on the loan agreement she made with the late George Carder of Warwick (Kent County, Rhode Island).[240] As executor of George Carder's estate, his kinsman John Carder contended he had tried unsuccessfully to collect from Eldridge the amount she owed George. That failure, he insisted to the court, constituted breach of promise. Thus, on January 20, 1835, two writs issued "for want of [the] body of Ellenor [*sic*] Eldridge" authorized and "command[ed]" Providence law enforcement to seize either the body of Eldridge or "the right title and interest" to Eldridge's Nathan Angell real estate lot measuring "fifty feet from & one hundred eighty feet back" as well as "the buildings & improvements thereon," consisting of "goods and chattels or Real Estate to the value of Eight Hundred dollars" (John Carder v. Elenor [*sic*] Eldridge, Court of Common Pleas, January 20, 1835). These references to Eldridge's "body" of goods and real estate—although in the context of a standard issue arrest warrant—nonetheless remind us of just how extensive was the property she had amassed. Additionally, on this matter, *Memoirs* indignantly complains that "all her [Eldridge's] families had been compelled to leave [her rental properties], at a single week's notice; and many of them, being unable to procure tenements, were compelled to find shelter in barns and out-houses, or even in the woods."[241] The publicity of the court case threatened wide exposure of plaintiff John Carder's allegation that Eldridge "ever . . . refused, and still doth refuse to pay the same." In turn, the case put her social character, her entrepreneurial success, and her livelihood at risk.[242]

The two court records dated January 20, 1835, had called for Providence law enforcement to arrest Elleanor Eldridge on the condition that "she be found in your precinct."[243] On one of these, Sherriff William B. Mann swore that he had been unable to locate Eldridge and so instead had alerted her tenants to her threatened situation. The authority to locate "lost" Native American women was integral to a legal colonial American phenomenon known as "warning out." Writing about eighteenth and nineteenth indigenous women "warned out" of New England towns, Herndon and Sekatau write, "Women who did not live in patriarchal households as daughters, wives, and mothers seemed 'out of place' to the town fathers, for they did not have male heads present to govern them. . . . Such independent women stirred fears of disorder in town officials wedded to their own customs and prompted their close attention."[244] Herndon and Sekatau's inference reasonably suggests that Eldridge's land disputes with white men were the result of Balch's and others' sexism, gynophobia, xenophobia, classism, and ethnocentrism. Eldridge's purported absence at the time might well have been an instance of her idiosyncratic subversion of white Rhode Island's system of "warning [indigenous people] out" of cities and towns as well as the reason she was away when Mann sold her land and dwellings to Balch. Herndon and Sekatau write, "Narragansett habits of travel and long-term visiting clashed with European concepts of 'belonging' to a particular place."[245] Eldridge, then, seems to have been doubly punished with land theft: on one hand for being out of (white) place when she visited her relatives and on the other hand for not conforming to conventional models of indigenous and African womanly behavior by living often among whites, living without patriarchal protection, and purchasing property. In addition, Herndon and Sekatau report, "as inhabitants of Rhode Island towns, native people who owned real estate were subject to paying taxes, just as the colonists were."[246] Documents dating from the late eighteenth century show some indigenous persons deliberately but temporarily moved around the state to have their uncollected taxes written off as "'bad rates' from time to time, when the collector advised that certain cases were not worth pursuing."[247]

According to Sidney S. Rider in his biographical sketch of Frances Whipple (McDougall), Eldridge "was not a woman who would submit quietly to such proceedings" as those initiated against her.[248] Eldridge's resistance to the injustice she faced demonstrated a strong arsenal comprised of some of Providence's most elite citizens. She was able, for example, to secure the legal assistance of Attorney General Albert C. Greene.[249] On April 19, 1836, she registered a formal complaint in the Providence Court of Common Pleas against a Benjamin Balch, charging him with "'Trespass and ejectment [sic],'" and seeking "to recover possession of certain close or parcel of land . . . on Spring Street" in Providence, along "with [the] dwelling house, outbuilding, & other improvements thereon."[250] On September 12, 1835, Balch, a white Providence baker, had purchased Eldridge's seized property after it had been confiscated in accordance with the writ dated January 26, 1835, because she had been unable to pay to recover it. Valued then with a taxable value of $4,000, that September the property had been sold to the highest bidder, to Balch.[251] As Jane Lancaster explains in "A Web of Iniquity?" Balch then paid off Carder and another creditor for their role in the fraudulent auction, "and obtained the property for a little under $1,700" (86). In April 1836, though, Eldridge demanded $3,000 in redress for personal injury; her lawsuit against Balch accused him of having "with force & arms" entered *two* of her real estate properties during the previous January, illegally forced her and her tenants (or relatives) from the premises, and brutalized them "all against the Peace, and to her great damage."[252] One extant court record dated January 24, 1836, summons Ben Lockwood and Henry Martin to appear at the end of November 1836 "to give evidence" in the trespass and ejection suit Eldridge had filed against Balch. Extant records of Eldridge contain no testimony from either Lockwood or Martin. On April 30, 1836, Eldridge prevailed as the state issued a legal writ for Balch's arrest in Providence and his subsequent appearance in court to pay the requisite $3,000 by the end of May 1836.[253]

Significantly, the *List of Persons Assessed in the City Tax . . . ordered by the [Providence] City Council, June 1836* identifies Benjamin Balch as a first-time tax payer for real estate holdings worth $2200; his name does not appear in Providence tax records before that year.[254] On the other hand, Elleanor Eldridge, who had been listed as a Providence real estate taxpayer since at least 1830, is conspicuously absent from the city's 1836 and 1837 tax records. Providence tax records document Eldridge's taxable real estate property as worth between $2,000 and $2,400 from 1838 to 1847.[255] After 1849, however, about two years after the last reprinting of *Memoirs*, her real estate property value rose dramatically from $3,200 to $4,800—evidence of the successes of both her adeptly argued lawsuits and her deft deployment of Whipple's adaptability as a biographer.

In the late eighteenth century and into the nineteenth, it was not uncommon for indigenous women to turn to US courts for justice.[256] Life writings of people of color often delineate court proceedings in which their (auto)biographical subjects have been involved. As Jeannine Marie DeLombard notes in *Slavery on Trial: Law, Abolitionism, and Print Culture*, multivalent details of legal cases provided early nineteenth-century black readers with vital information about the workings of the courts system and inspired their use of it.[257] Including details about Eldridge's cases in *Memoirs* enables Whipple and Eldridge not only to inspire "the colored population" of Providence to emulate Eldridge's industry as "the writer" asserts in the biography's preface, but it also demonstrates some actions people of color could take in their own defense, ways they could also replicate Eldridge's courageous determination to fight within the constraints of the law to regain her property.[258] Besides New England's women of color plaintiffs in court petitions and freedom suits, formerly enslaved New Yorker Isabella Baumfree—self-named Sojourner Truth in 1843—had used the courts to recover her abducted son Peter in 1828.[259] In 1835, Truth again successfully used the courts to sue Benjamin and Ann Folger, who threatened her livelihood as a cook for hire when they circulated a libelous rumor that Truth had poisoned them. In addition, Truth further pled her innocence of the Folgers' accusation by relying on "a book written by British-born newspaper editor Gilbert Vale, who based the volume on interviews he had conducted with her [Truth], as a means of getting her side of the story before the public."[260]

Following such cases as the 1780's suit of Belinda [Royall] for reparations in Massachusetts and Truth's reliance on (elite whites' dependence on) print culture, Eldridge used *Memoirs* to argue dimensions that could not or would not surface about her virtues in Rhode Island courts.[261] Furthermore, Eldridge, like Truth, used a white woman's narrativization of her life to safeguard real estate property; according to Jean M. Humez, "It was to help pay the mortgage on [Truth's] house, probably at the suggestion of William Lloyd Garrison, that [Truth] sought the aid of Olive Gilbert."[262] Just as Truth spoke her truth to Vale, Gilbert, and other interlocutors, Eldridge protested the seizure of her property both to Whipple and to the magistrates of the lawsuits in which she was involved.[263] Throughout her trials, legal and otherwise, Eldridge resisted unjust harassment and ultimately retained both her real estate and her rights. No doubt a combination of grit, perspicacity, and tenacity were required for Eldridge to maintain what Rohrbach has called a "real estate empire" across multiple cities in Rhode Island.[264]

Conclusion: *Memoirs Of Elleanor Eldridge* As African American Literature

Trying to unlock the racialized aspects of the complications and complexities of *Memoirs of Elleanor Eldridge* without a key, readers might overlook its value and function as African American literature: this text, too, expresses black literary, linguistic, and oral power, sharing rhetorical tropes with, and joining various African autobiographical traditions in the US represented by, an enormous body of literary works, including *The Interesting Narrative of the Life of Olaudah Equiano, or Gustavus Vassa, the African* (1791), *The Life and Religious Experience of Jarena Lee, a Coloured Lady, Giving an Account of Her Call to Preach the Gospel* (1836), and Harriet Jacobs's anonymously published *Incidents in the Life of a Slave Girl, Written by Herself* (1861). *Memoirs of Elle-anor Eldridge* proves an effective collaboration between a narrating black and indigenous woman and the white woman interlocutor she selected to pen her story. We misapprehend the power of black orature and black expressivity when we naively attribute the authority and elo-quence of *Memoirs of Elleanor Eldridge* only to Whipple and contend Eldridge "might have died in obscurity and poverty had not a group of white women, led by Frances Whipple . . . decided to help her."[265] We underestimate the force of the women's interracial collaboration, and worse, the profundity of Eldridge's self-determination when we dis-count Eldridge's assertion of choice and voice in all aspects of *Memoirs*.

Reflecting on Whipple and Eldridge as elders, Rider wrote: "Elleanor recovered her property after paying pretty heavily for it, and lived to a good old age, a respected and respectable colored woman, tall and erect in her 80th year as the young oak in the native forests of Rhode Island, through which her grandmother had wandered among the last of a race now unknown."[266] Providence *Births, Marriages, and Deaths* lists Eldridge's death date as June 24, 1862, and Rhode Island histor-ical archives verify the lands and legacy she left her heirs.[267] Further-more, she left them the right of pride in her tenacity, in her willing-ness to press her cases—and to continue to do so when other persons would have forsaken them, particularly given that the courts and the era in which she was forced to press her claims were infamously racist, white supremacist. Most crucially, the historical record and *Memoirs* speak to Eldridge's extraordinary access as one singled out for success. The family of her distant kinsman William J. Brown suffered a simi-larly appalling land theft, and yet they did not share Eldridge's oppor-tunities for legal redress; consequently, Brown's autobiography nar-rates a different, more embittered story. *Memoirs* speaks passionately to Eldridge's determination—and her ability to marshal powerful friends. But it speaks as well to the unbridled racism and intersectional oppres-sion of the time.

Dispelling persistent myths about Elleanor Eldridge and other women of color born nominally free in the first generations of post-emancipation New England depends on continued recuperations and investigations of their lives. Without contextualizing analyses, harmful myths about them abound, leaving intact erroneous notions that people of color had no agency and formed no social, political, or ideological coalitions among themselves in defiance of systemic, racialized discriminations against them. Such myths deny Eldridge's actual and figurative descendants legitimate pride in this ancestor. Too many Americans are generally ignorant about the experience of *any* women of color in early national courts, and that ignorance means that misconceptions remain about legal institutions and court practices of early nineteenth-century Rhode Island. In addition, most Americans are generally ignorant of Elleanor Eldridge's life, her property ownership, and her strategic exploitation of US white (women's) social activism and *belles lettres*, despite the numerous editions of the *two* Eldridge biographies reissued within a nine-year stretch (at least) and marked in part by a rapid development gained by black people, indigenous populations, and mixed race persons of their printing ways, means, and media as well as an increase of each group's respective usages of mainstream print media. Without attending to Eldridge, we continue to perpetuate myths of the pathetic limitations of women of color in US courts without also acknowledging their triumphant reaches. A focus inclusive of their legal exonerations together with exposure of the abuses of judicial power over them reshape the history of women of color as participants in the early national legal system. In addition, such studies reshape understandings of black and indigenous resistance to white hegemony. People of color launched individual and collective resistance to social, economic, and gender oppressions that threatened their political and cultural mores as well as their socioeconomic achievements in New England. Though that resistance sometimes failed to protect them, at other times it succeeded. Elleanor Eldridge ultimately prevailed.

Notes

1   Elleanor Eldridge and Frances H. Whipple, *Memoirs of Elleanor Eldridge* (Providence: B. T. Albro, 1838), 46–47. All references to *Memoirs of Elleanor Eldridge* are based on the 1838 edition, reprinted in this volume.

2   Edward Hayes O'Neill, *A History of American Biography, 1800–1935* (Philadelphia: University of Pennsylvania Press, 1935), 16.

3   The National Union Catalog, Pre-1956 Imprints lists no printing of either Eldridge biography in 1844. *Memoirs* was one of only six books by US women of African descent included in the Woman's Building Library of the 1893 World's Columbian Exposition. Library of Congress and American Library Association, Committee on Resources of American Libraries, National Union Catalog Subcommittee, *The National Union Catalog, Pre-1956 Imprints; a Cumulative Author List Representing Library of Congress Printed Cards and Titles Reported by Other American Libraries,* 754 vols. (London: Mansell, 1968). According to Amina Gautier, it was rare in that context, too, in that more than seven thousand volumes were exhibited in the Women's Building. "African American Women's Writings in the Woman's Building Library," *Libraries & Culture* 41, no. 1 (2006): 57. See "List of Books Sent by Home and Foreign Committees to the Library of the Woman's Building, World's Columbian Exposition, Chicago, 1893," Page 53, col. 1, University of Pennsylvania, accessed March 11, 2013, http://digital.library. upenn.edu/women/clarke/library/library.html

4   Sidney S. Rider writes, "Mr. [Rufus W.] Griswold, in his notice of Mrs. [Frances Whipple] Greene, in his *Female Poets of America*, states that 30,000 copies of this (first) memoir [*Memoirs of Elleanor Eldridge*] was sold, and Allibone has copied from Griswold. Doubtless there were a considerable number, but not nearly as many as 30,000. It is questionable whether there were more than three editions of the first one, and there is certainly but one edition of the second one. An edition of a Rhode Island book numbering 10,000 or 15,000 would be an extraordinary thing, altogether unknown. Both these little books were printed by Mr. B. T. Albro, of course on hand presses, for at that time such a thing as a power book printing press was unknown in Providence." *Bibliographical Memoirs of Three Rhode Island Authors: Joseph B. Argall, Frances H. (Whipple) Mcdougall, Catharine R. Williams* (n.p.: 1880), 37–38. Rider gives the dates of three editions of *Memoirs of Elleanor Eldridge* as 1838, 1840, and 1842. He is incorrect at least in the number of editions of *Elleanor's Second Book* that were printed. The first appeared in 1839, and Albro printed a second edition in 1842.

5   See the Black Heritage Library Collection's 1971 reprint of the second edition of *Memoirs of Elleanor Eldridge*. Frances H. Green [Whipple] and Elleanor Eldridge, *Memoirs of Elleanor Eldridge*, 2nd ed., The Black Heritage Library Collection (Freeport, NY: Books for Libraries Press, 1971). Minor corrections were made, however, to editions reprinted between 1840 and 1847.

6   Dorothy Sterling, *We Are Your Sisters: Black Women in the Nineteenth Century* (New York: W. W. Norton, 1984); and Darlene Clark Hine and Kathleen Thompson, *A Shining Thread of Hope: The History of Black Women in America* (New York: Broadway, 1998).

7   Xiomara Santamarina, "Review of Harriet Wilson's New England: Race, Writing and Region," *Legacy* 25, no. 2 (2008): 338–39.

8   John Ernest, *Chaotic Justice: Rethinking African American Literary History* (Chapel Hill: University of North Carolina Press, 2009), 111.

9   I read *Memoirs of Elleanor Eldridge* as African American literature following the argument of Frances Smith Foster and Kim D. Green that African American written literature "includes writings by African Americans that are directed to or even mediated by people with cultural traditions that do not have African or even American origins, but it privileges literature published by African Americans for African Americans and generally about African Americans." "Ports of Call, Pulpits of Consultation," *A Companion to African American Literature*, ed. Gene Andrew Jarrett (Chichester, UK: Wiley-Blackwell, 2010), 45–46.

10   See Jack D. Forbes for fuller discussion of the seven different identificatory terms applied to early New England populations: *Africans and Native Americans: The Language of Race and the Evolution of Red-Black Peoples*, 2nd ed. (Urbana: University of Illinois Press, 1993), 212 *passim*. According to Ruth Wallis Herndon and Ella Wilcox Sekatau, "Indians were counted as 'Blacks'" as early as 1750. See their provocative argument that white Rhode Island's bigoted redesignation of indigenous people as "black," especially after 1780, was one more way "to deny the existence of people with any claim to the land"; that is, the racial reduction to "black" legalized land theft and dispossession. Ruth Wallis Herndon and Ella Wilcox Sekatau, "The Right to a Name: The Narragansett People and Rhode Island Officials in the Revolutionary Era," *Ethnohistory* 44, no. 3 (1997): 457n33, 453.

11   Joanne Pope Melish, "Recovering (from) Slavery: Four Struggles to Tell the Truth," in *Slavery and Public History: The Tough Stuff of American Memory*, ed. James O. Horton and Lois E. Horton (New York: New Press, 2006), 126.

12   Quigley and Finkelman, "Rhode Island," 41. It is not clear whether any of the persons listed in Nelson B. Eldred and Walter Steesy's *Robert Eldred* are people of color or bear any relation to Elleanor Eldridge and her family. *Robert Eldred (Eldredge) of Yarmouth and Chatham, Cape Cod, Massachusetts and Some of His Descendants* (Interlaken, NY: Heart of the Lakes, 1996). Cf. Barbara Picard Chadwick, *Eldredge: Harwich to Haverhill: Being Notes on the Early Eldredge Generations and Direct Descendants of Robert Eldred(Ge) of Chatham and Charwich and through William, William, Isaac, Isaac, Jr., Samuel and Cyrus* (West Boxford, MA: B. P. Chadwick, 1988).

13   Cf. Jean Pfaelzer, "Hanging Out: A Research Methodology," *Legacy: A Journal of American Women Writers* 27, no. 1 (2010): 140–60.

14   Direct quotations from Eldridge's biography are based on the 1838 edition of *Memoirs of Elleanor Eldridge*, reprinted in full in this volume, unless otherwise noted.

15   Eldridge and Whipple, *Memoirs*, 99. Whipple expressed her exoticization of Rhode Island's indigenous peoples in *Namuntenoo*, which Rider describes as "a legend of the Narragansetts, in six cantos, three of which, according to [Griswold], were published in Philadelphia in 1840." Rider quotes Griswold's appreciation of the poem as follows: "In the delineation of Indian character and adventure can be seen the fruits of intelligent study, and a nice apprehension of the influence of external nature in psychological development." Rider, *Bibliographical Memoirs*, 43.

16   Eldridge and Whipple, *Memoirs*, 104.

17   Eldridge and Whipple, *Memoirs*, 103. The first *Robert* Eldridge cited in the Rhode Island census is listed in 1790, but he is recorded as a white male living at North Kingston (Washington County) with another white male and two white females. Heritagequestonline.com. HeritageQuest Online lists only one *Robin* Eldridge in nineteenth-century Rhode Island census data: the 1800 report cites a "Robin Eldridge, Black" living in Warwick (Kent County). No other Roberts or Robins appear in the Rhode Island census until 1860, which lists the Robert M. Eldridge cited above (mulatto, aged 50). The 1860 Warwick record lists this man as a head of household and farm laborer with real estate amounting to $1,000. A second Robert Eldridge, also "mulatto," is listed as twelve years old. Neither of these Robert Eldridges appears in the 1870 census.

18   Forbes, *Africans and Native Americans*, 262–63.

19   Forbes, *Africans and Native Americans*, 212.

20   This reprint of *Memoirs of Elleanor Eldridge* recovers Eldridge to African American literary history but not to Native American literary history, in part because the white supremacist history of Rhode Island has made investigation into Eldridge's indigenous heritages difficult to conduct. Where we perceive differences between markers of African traditions and those of Native traditions in *Memoirs*, the biography details so little of indigeneity that distinguishing Native American cultural influences on Eldridge's life poses a significant challenge. My goal to situate Eldridge among the first freeborn black Rhode Islanders does not result from the optic "evidence" of *Memoirs*'s frontispiece portrait so much as from what P. Gabrielle Foreman rightly calls "a historically rooted epistemology grounded in collective experience and expertise . . . [and reflection] upon the *social* body . . . the body's signs in relation to a larger body politic that has historically relegated the evidence of consanguineous relations to the realm of Blackness." P. Gabrielle Foreman, *Activist Sentiments: Reading Black Women in the Nineteenth Century* (Urbana: University of Illinois Press, 2009), 137. One goal of this reprinted edition is to inspire Native Americanists and others to research Eldridge further, to expand knowledge of her, and thus to enable deeper appreciation for her biographies and her nineteenth-century social and cultural contexts.

21   Eldridge and Whipple, *Memoirs*, 93. I make this claim in spite of the narrator's identification of herself as first-person singular author in the preface to the first edition. Whipple's authorship is never explicitly identified in the biography, in part, as Whipple's biographers presume, to honor *Memoirs of Elleanor Eldridge* as a "work of charity" (Rider, qtd. in O'Dowd, 63). That Whipple wrote *Memoirs of Elleanor Eldridge* has been further established by contemporary advertisements for the biography she placed in periodicals such as the *Liberator*.

22   Elleanor Eldridge and Frances H. Whipple (Green), *Elleanor's Second Book* (Providence: B. T. Albro, 1839).

23   For an analysis of *Elleanor's Second Book*, see Joycelyn Moody, "Frances

Whipple, Elleanor Eldridge, and the Politics of Interracial Collaboration," *American Literature* 83, no. 4 (2011): 689–717.

24   Anthony Appiah and Henry Louis Gates, Jr., eds., *Africana: The Encyclopedia of the African and African American Experience*, 2nd ed. (New York: Oxford University Press, 2005), 2:525.

25   Robert J. Cottrol, "Law, Politics, and Race in Urban America: Towards a New Synthesis," *Rutgers Law Journal* 17 (1985–1986): 486.

26   Baumfree/Truth (b. 1799?) was freed from bondage in New York in 1827.

27   Foster and Green, "Ports of Call," 47–48.

28   Eve Allegra Raimon, "Lost and Found: Making Claims on Archives," *Legacy: A Journal of American Women Writers* 27, no. 2 (2010): 260.

29   Marianne Hirsch defines postmemory as "not a movement, method, or idea; I see it, rather, as a structure of inter- and trans-generational transmission of traumatic knowledge and experience. It is a consequence of traumatic recall but (unlike post-traumatic stress disorder) at a generational remove." "The Generation of Postmemory," *Poetics Today* 29, no. 1 (2008): 106.

30   Robin Eldridge seems like one of the black soldiers such as Nathaniel Jones, whom Ruth Wallis Herndon describes in *Unwelcome Americans*—"a free Negro man": "On 4 January 1781 Nathaniel Jones had enlisted in the Rhode Island Regiment for the town of Johnston, tempted by the lucrative bounty the voters offered: one hundred silver dollars, almost a year's wages for an unskilled laboring man. In 1781, such payments were the only way reluctant men could be persuaded to join the Continental Army." Ruth Wallis Herndon, *Unwelcome Americans: Living on the Margin in Early New England* (Philadelphia: University of Pennsylvania Press, 2001), 37.

31   Five Prophets appear in the 1800 census: Chloe, John, Peter, and Peter, all living in Providence County; a Watt Prophet is listed as living in Warwick. In 1810, there is only one Peter listed, and he is identified as B[lack]. The only other Prophet listed that year is a Martha (or Marthas, Marthias, or Mathias?). I found three black Prophets (of five total) in the 1860 census, all living in Warwick (Kent County), Rhode Island: Mary C., age 42; Nancy, age 44; and Thomas, age 40. By 1870, there are nine Prophets listed, and only one is identified as white, another M[ulatto], and the other seven black. No racial designations provided are for the nine Prophets listed in the 1820 census. http://persi.heritagequestonline.com.libweb.lib.utsa.edu/hqoweb/library/do/census/search/basic. *Memoirs of Elleanor Eldridge* states that Elleanor and George had two cousins named Jeremiah and Lucy Prophet living in Warwick around 1832. Eldridge and Whipple, *Memoirs*, 135.

32   Among the crucial areas of research yet to be done on Eldridge include an analysis of her real estate property using Geographic Information Systems such as that Cameron B. Blevins has completed using extant deeds to the land owned by Venture Smith. Blevins's work on Smith reveals that analyses of Eldridge's lands and deeds using GIS

would provide rich insight into Eldridge's decisions as an entrepreneur, neighbor, resident-worker, and family member. See Blevins, "'Owned by Negro Venture': Land and Liberty in the Life of Venture Smith," *Venture Smith and the Business of Slavery and Freedom*, ed. James Brewer Stewart (Amherst: University of Massachusetts Press, 2010), 129–59.

33   In contrast to Eldridge's property tax report, the *Valuation of Taxable Property, in the Town of Warwick, as apportioned by the assessors of taxes, February 7th, A.D. 1856*, lists a James N. Carder of the Old Warwick District as owning real estate property worth $1800 and $300 worth of personal property. *Valuation of Taxable Property, in the Town of Warwick, as apportioned by the assessors of taxes, February 7th, A.D. 1856* (Providence: Sayles, Miller, and Simons, 1856). The 1856 *Valuation of Taxable Property* further reveals the taxes paid on personal and/or real estate property by several very wealthy Carders located in the Apponaug District (central Warwick), including John (possessing $2,500 in personal wealth and no real estate); James (possessing $2,000 worth of real estate property and no personal property of taxable value); and Randall (owner of $8,000 in real estate property and $4000 of taxable personal property). Carder women paying taxes listed in the 1856 *Valuation of Taxable Property, in the Town of Warwick* include Sarah and Jane (possessing $800 and $1,000 respectively, in taxable real estate property; neither held personal property sufficient to be taxed). Among the Eldridges recorded in the 1856 *Valuation*, Elenor [or Elleanor] Eldridge's name is followed by a Sarah P. Eldridge (widow), taxed on $1,500 of real estate property. The disparity between Sarah P. Eldridge's $1500 real estate wealth and Elleanor's own $600 may indicate that the widowed Sarah's greater wealth ensued from her marriage to a white man, whereas Elleanor Eldridge, biracial and apparently never married, remarkably was nearly as wealthy as Sarah Carder. *Valuation of Taxable Property*, 4, 11–12. Cf. Loren Schweninger, "Property Owning Free African-American Women in the South, 1800–1870," *Journal of Women's History* 1, no. 3 (1990): 13–44.

34   Eldridge and Whipple, *Memoirs*, 145.

35   DoVeanna S. Fulton, *Speaking Power: Black Feminist Orality in Women's Narratives of Slavery* (Albany: State University of New York Press, 2006), xi.

36   Edward Hayes O'Neill, *A History*, 9.

37   Lydia Maria Child, *Celebrated Women: Or, Biographies of Good Wives* (New York: C. S. Francis, 1858), 9–10.

38   Eldridge and Whipple, *Elleanor's Second Book*, 27–28.

39   Eldridge and Whipple, *Memoirs*, 145. Ironically, representing people of color a generation later than persons Ruth Wallis Herndon examines in "Literacy among New England's Transient Poor, 1750–1800," Eldridge defies Herndon's conclusion that literacy and property ownership (and wealth and transience) are generally positively correlated. Ruth Wallis Herndon, "Literacy among New England's Transient Poor, 1750–1800," *Journal of Social History* 29, no. 4 (1996): 963–965.

40   See Kristina Bross and Hilary E. Wyss on indigenous persons in colonial New England who made conscious, informed uses of material and "print" texts, including

one eighteenth-century Native American woman who (perhaps subversively and derisively) lined her woven basket with an outdated local newspaper. Kristina Bross and Hilary E. Wyss, eds. *Early Native Literacies in New England: A Documentary and Critical Anthology* (Amherst: University of Massachusetts Press, 2008).

41   DoVeanna S. Fulton Minor and Reginald Pitts, *Speaking Lives, Authoring Texts: Three African American Women's Oral Slave Narratives* (Albany: State University of New York Press, 2010), 3.

42   John Ernest discusses this idea broadly in "African American Literature and the Abolitionist Movement, 1845 to the Civil War," in *The Cambridge History of African American Literature*, ed. Maryemma Graham and Jerry Washington Ward (New York: Cambridge University Press, 2010), 91–115.

43   White power over black texts forms the focus of Vincent Carretta's "The Emergence of an African American Literary Canon, 1760–1820," in *The Cambridge History of African American Literature*, 52–65.

44   Fulton, *Speaking Power*; Jean Humez, "Reading the Narrative of Sojourner Truth as a Collaborative Text," *Frontiers* 16, no. 1 (1996): 43–44.

45   William L. Andrews, *To Tell a Free Story: The First Century of Afro-American Autobiography, 1760–1865* (Urbana: University of Illinois Press, 1986), 33.

46   Humez, "Reading," 30.

47   Fulton, *Speaking Power*, 13.

48   Fulton, *Speaking Power*, 12–13.

49   Quoted in Fulton, *Speaking Power*, 110.

50   Fulton Minor and Pitts, *Speaking Lives*, 3.

51   Fulton Minor and Pitts, *Speaking Lives*, 12.

52   Eldridge and Whipple, *Memoirs*, 111.

53   Frances Smith Foster, "Creative Collaboration: As African American As Sweet Potato Pie," in *Post-Bellum, Pre-Harlem: African American Literature and Culture, 1877–1919*, ed. Barbara McCaskill and Caroline Gebhard (New York: New York University Press, 2006), 17–33.

54   Brown might have been Eldridge's kinsman, as the life writing produced by each autobiographer names Chloe Prophet as an ancestor. See Joanne Pope Melish, introduction to *The Life of William J. Brown of Providence, R.I.: With Personal Recollections of Incidents in Rhode Island*, ed. Rosalind Cobb Wiggins and Joanne Pope Melish (Durham: University of New Hampshire Press, 2006), xvi–xvii, xxii–xxiii. Notably, Eldridge and Brown do not mention one another in their respective life narratives.

55   Elizabeth McHenry, *Forgotten Readers: Recovering the Lost History of African American Literary Societies* (Durham, NC: Duke University Press, 2002), 17.

56   See Roy E. Finkenbine, "Belinda," in *Encyclopedia of African American History, 1619–1895: From the Colonial Period to the Age of Frederick Douglass*, ed. Paul Finkelman (New York: Oxford University Press, 2006), 1:123; and Carretta, "Emergence," 62.

57   David N. Gellman, "Race, the Public Sphere, and Abolition in Late Eighteenth-Century New York," *Journal of the Early Republic* 20, no. 4 (2000): 630–31.

58   For more on Jackson and Thompson, see Fulton Minor and Pitts, *Speaking Lives*.

59   Cf. Candice Love Jackson for a discussion of altogether different "[c]ollaborations between [twentieth- and twenty-first-century] authors within the African American literary tradition." "From Writer to Reader: Black Popular Fiction," in *The Cambridge History of African American Literature*, 655–79.

60   According to William L. Andrews, most black slave narratives at the end of the eighteenth century were (white-authored) "confessions of condemned black felons." Andrews, *To Tell*, 33.

61   Joycelyn Moody, "African American Women and the United States Slave Narrative," in *The Cambridge Companion to African American Women's Literature*, ed. Angelyn Mitchell and Danille K. Taylor (Cambridge: Cambridge University Press, 2009), 109–127; qtd. passage at 110.

62   David Quigley and Paul Finkelman, "Rhode Island," in *Encyclopedia of African American History, 1619–1895: From the Colonial Period to the Age of Frederick Douglass*, ed. Paul Finkelman (New York: Oxford University Press, 2006), 3:41. In "Using the Testimony of Ex-Slaves: Approaches and Problems" (1975), prominent historian John Blassingame has also written misleadingly about the genre and rhetoric of *Memoirs of Elleanor Eldridge*, asserting, "[Certain] features are so prevalent in the narratives of Elleanor Eldridge, Sally Williams, Jane Blake, and others that they generally reveal few of the details of slave life." Quoted in Charles T. Davis and Henry Louis Gates, Jr., eds., *The Slave's Narrative* (Oxford: Oxford University Press, 1985), 82.

63   Vincent Carretta has suggested that there are two possible persons who might have been the Elisha Niles, as well as a Charles Holt, who served as Venture Smith's amanuensis (181n3, 165, 175). See Carretta, "Venture Smith: One of a Kind," in *Venture Smith and the Business of Slavery and Freedom*.

64   Venture Smith and Elisha Niles, *A Narrative of the Life and Adventures of Venture, a Native of Africa: But Resident above Sixty Years in the United States of America. Related by Himself* (New London: Printed by C. Holt, 1798). Paul E. Lovejoy, "The African Background of Venture Smith," *Venture Smith and the Business of Slavery and Freedom*, 35.

65   David Quigley, "Venture Smith," in *Encyclopedia of African American History, 1619–1895: From the Colonial Period to the Age of Frederick Douglass*, ed. Paul Finkelman (New York: Oxford University Press, 2006), 3:170. Lovejoy gives a fascinating account of Niles's apparent attempts to transcribe Smith's speech phonetically in 1798—an endeavor later "corrected" in the edition of the *Narrative* owned by Yale University; see Lovejoy, 39.

66   Andrews, *To Tell*, 42.

67   Smith and Niles, *A Narrative*, iii; Andrews, *To Tell*, 33.

68   Andrews, *To Tell*, 42.

69   Carretta, "Emergence," 54–56. In "Venture Smith: One of a Kind," Carretta writes: "Venture's willingness to resist slavery physically, his refusal to wait for emancipation in the afterlife, and his skepticism about 'white' Christianity did anticipate significant aspects of nineteenth-century slave narratives, exemplified by Frederick Douglass's *Narrative* (1845). But Smith's *Narrative* apparently did so without influencing later narratives, at least in part because in 1798 it was published only in Connecticut, and preprinted only there in 1835 and 1897. It was not included in nineteenth-century abolitionist anthologies, perhaps in part because . . . it is ideologically so different from other works by authors of African descent" (164). See Carretta in *Venture Smith and the Business of Slavery and Freedom*. Andrews concludes that the end of Smith's *Narrative* portrays Smith as a miserable elder "without power, community, or religious faith to assuage his sense of alienation, [but] Smith could yet draw consolation from his love for his wife, his conviction of his own integrity, and, above all, his freedom." *To Tell*, 52. Interestingly, Eldridge comes to a very different close in *Elleanor's Second Book*, which depicts her as having regained her real estate property but still without romance or more than nominal freedom.

70   Harriet E. Wilson, *Our Nig, or, Sketches from the Life of a Free Black*, ed. P. Gabrielle Foreman and Reginald H. Pitts (1865; repr. New York: Penguin Books, 2009).

71   B[enjamin] B. Thatcher, *Memoir of Phillis Wheatley, a Native African and a Slave* (Boston, New York: G. W. Light; Moore and Payne etc., 1834). Thatcher does not mention Wheatley's conversion to Christianity—an irony since so many literary critics have emphasized the religious and theological precepts in Wheatley's poems. For a discussion of Wheatley's Christian piety, see Vincent Carretta, *Phillis Wheatley: Biography of a Genius in Bondage* (Athens: University of Georgia Press, 2011), 162–165.

72   [Mary Prince,] *The History of Mary Prince, A West Indian Slave, Related by Herself* (1831), in *Six Women's Slave Narratives*, ed. William L. Andrews (New York: Oxford University Press, 1988).

73   Stefan M. Wheelock, "Dividing a Nation, Uniting a People: African American Literature and the Abolitionist Movement," in *The Cambridge History of African American Literature*, 66–90.

74   See Wheelock, "Dividing," 81.

75   Sandra Pouchet Paquet, "Mary Prince," in *The Oxford Companion to African American Literature*, ed. William L. Andrews, Frances Smith Foster, and Trudier Harris (New York: Oxford University Press, 1997), 599.

76   The preface to the biography is notably longer and remarkably different in second and subsequent editions of *Memoirs of Elleanor Eldridge*. The 1838 preface appears on Eldridge and Whipple, *Memoirs*, 93.

77   Eldridge and Whipple, *Memoirs*, 93.

78   Eldridge and Whipple, *Memoirs*, 93.

79   Eldridge and Whipple, *Memoirs*, 93.

80   Eldridge and Whipple, *Memoirs*, 93.

81   Eldridge and Whipple, *Memoirs*, 110.

82   According to *Memoirs*, Christopher died at sea. On the frequency of men of African descent "coasting," or seafaring, to earn a living—and the high mortality rates seamen suffered—see W. Jeffrey Bolster, *Black Jacks: African American Seamen in the Age of Sail* (Cambridge: Harvard University Press, 1997).

83   Pamela Newkirk, ed., *Letters from Black America* (New York: Farrar, Straus, and Giroux, 2009), 61.

84   I have elsewhere discussed parallels between *Memoirs* and early American women's fiction. See Joycelyn Moody and Sarah R. Robbins, "Seeking Trust and Commitment in Women's Interracial Collaborations in the Nineteenth Century and Today," *MELUS* 38, no. 1 (Spring 2013): 50–75.

85   Cf. Jean Humez's account of the tense exchange in Gilbert's *Narrative of Sojourner Truth* to represent Truth as an enslaved mother victimized through rape to become a mother then neglectful of the children she bore from those rapes; Humez asserts that the two women clearly had conflicting perspectives and divergent "assumptions about [Truth's] responsibilities as a mother." "Reading," 43.

86   Susanna Haswell Rowson, *Charlotte Temple*, ed. Cathy N. Davidson (1794; repr. New York: Oxford University Press, 1986); Hannah Webster Foster, Henry Wysham Lanier, and American Imprint Collection (Library of Congress), *The Coquette; Or, The History of Liza Wharton; A Novel; Founded on Fact* (Boston: Printed by Samuel Etheridge for E. Larkin, 1797).

87   Humez, "Reading," 30.

88   Eldridge and Whipple, *Memoirs*, 104. Joseph Baker is listed in the 1810 Rhode Island census as residing at both Warwick (Kent County) and the South District of Providence.

89   Eldridge and Whipple, *Memoirs*, 104.

90   The second instantiation of Eldridge's speech appears in a private, familial scene in chapter 2, in which her younger brother "sprung to his sister's arms, and clinging around her neck, cried 'Don't go, Nelly!'" Instead of reconstructing Eldridge's reply in direct discourse, the narrator reports that "Elleanor . . . comforted him with the promise of coming back soon." Eldridge and Whipple, *Memoirs*, 106.

91   Eldridge and Whipple, *Memoirs*, 110. See Fulton on the power of both orality and silence in *Louisa Picquet, the Octoroon*, by Hiram Mattison, and mediated slave narratives (*Speaking Power*, especially 11–15).

92   For more on these letters, see Joycelyn Moody, "Intimacy and Interlocution in Early Rhode Island," in *African American Women's Language*, ed. Sonja Lanehart (Cambridge: Cambridge Scholars, 2009), 212–27.

93   Raimon, "Lost and Found," 261.

94   Humez, "Reading," 40.

95   Grey Gundaker, "Give Me a Sign: African Americans, Print, and Practice," in *An Extensive Republic: Print, Culture, and Society in the New Nation, 1790–1840*, ed.

Robert A. Gross and Mary Kelley (Chapel Hill: University of North Carolina Press, 2010), 2:484–5.

96   Sarah C. O'Dowd, *A Rhode Island Original: Frances Harriet Whipple Green McDougall* (Hanover, NH: University Press of New England, 2004). Most of the details about Whipple's life reconstructed here are based on Sarah C. O'Dowd's biography. O'Dowd acknowledges the limitations of her biography, asserting in her preface that "even the census takers seem to have missed her [Frances Whipple], and she was seldom mentioned in other Rhode Island documents," other than official records and a few regional newspapers (xii).

97   O'Dowd, *A Rhode Island Original*, 2.

98   O'Dowd, *A Rhode Island Original*, 5.

99   Rider, *Biographical Memoirs*, 29.

100   Rider, *Biographical Memoirs*, 31.

101   Rider, *Biographical Memoirs*, 35. Whipple contributed a number of signed and initialled poems to the 1840 collection *The Envoy*, the title page of which does not identify either author or editor. Its preface, however, comprised of a long poem titled "The Charge" (v–vi), is signed "F.H.W." Frances H. [Whipple] Green, *The Envoy. From Free Hearts to the Free* (Pawtucket, RI: Juvenile Eman. Society, 1840). This poem calls women to become authors, asking, "When woman's form is sunk into the brute, / Shall woman's pen be still—her voice be mute?" (ll. 27–28). In addition, "The Western Fold, an Allegory" is signed fully "Frances Harriet Whipple" (69–84).

102   Rider, *Biographical Memoirs*, 32.

103   Rider, *Biographical Memoirs*, 32.

104   Rider, *Biographical Memoirs*, 32.

105   O'Dowd, *A Rhode Island Original*, 59, 79. On the many variations of Whipple's literary names, including pseudonyms and noms de plume, see O'Dowd, xiii and xviii. Creating especial confusion for contemporary researchers is Whipple's last surname, about which O'Dowd contends: "Genealogical evidence points to 'McDougal' [i.e., one *l*] as the spelling of the name of Frances's second husband, and this was probably also the spelling she adopted as his wife. It appears that around 1875, most publishers began to emend this spelling to 'McDougall'" (xviii).

106   *The Wampanoag, and Operatives' Journal*. O'Dowd describes this publication as "a non-political magazine dedicated to the interests of the Fall River [Massachusetts] mill operatives" in southern New England (65).Whipple (Green) is accepted as author of the 345-page novel *Might and Right*, published "by a Rhode Islander" in 1844. The frontispiece to *Might and Right* is a detailed engraving from a daguerreotype of Dorr, inscribed as "Inaugurated Governor of Rhode Island / May 3d 1842." Whipple Green confirms her devotion to the Dorrite movement with the book's dedication: "To Thomas Wilson Dorr, The True and Tried Patriot, the fearless Defender of Human Rights, this work is respectfully inscribed by the / The [*sic*] Author." Frances H. Green, *Might and Right* (Providence: A. H. Stillwell, 1844). Her support of Dorr as a political

candidate is notable, for his white rank-and-file supporters "were hostile to black suffrage." Quigley and Finkelman, "Rhode Island," 42. Conversely, her support is unsurprising in that "Dorr was a committed abolitionist" (42). According to Quigley and Finkelman, in the years that Eldridge and Whipple produced the second editions of the Eldridge biographies, "from 1840 to 1842 blacks participated in the Rhode Island Suffrage Association, a white-dominated organization dedicated to eliminating property requirements for voting" (42). Dorr, a Democrat, was the leader of this organization. The suffrage movement led to "the Dorr war" and ended with the 1843 constitution that immediately freed from slavery all (mostly elderly) persons still bound. In addition, 300 black voting men threw their support behind Dorr's Whig opponent, demonstrating their considerable political clout. In 1857 the black vote was sufficiently strong to elect a black man, Thomas Howland, to the office of election warden. Quigley and Finkelman, "Rhode Island," 42.

107   O'Dowd speculates, in email correspondence with one of her sources, that Brittain's wife may have been Catherine Lyon, formerly of Providence. *A Rhode Island Original*, 102n5.

108   Regarding the genre of *Beyond the Veil*, Rider reports that he follows the account of Rufus W. Griswold, in *The Female Poets of America* (Philadelphia: Carey and Hart, 1849): Whipple [as Mrs. McDougall] claimed to have been visited by "a spirit voice . . . from Randolph" who directed her to "write for me." She finally consented, but supposed it was only to write a small pamphlet until at length was told that it was to be a book" (Rider, *Bibliographical Memoirs*, 45–46). Ultimately, she produced an article.

109   Gundaker, "Give Me a Sign," 484.

110   Quoted in Joanna Brooks, Lisa L. Moore, and Caroline Wigginton, eds., *Transatlantic Feminisms in the Age of Revolutions* (New York: Oxford University Press, 2011), 135. Also, as Loren Schweninger observes about Eldridge's southern counterparts, "For a variety of reasons, property owning free black women remained circumspect about committing themselves to marriage. Those who had saved some money, acquired real estate, or operated a business could lose everything by the wrong choice of a mate since the courts invariably recognized the property rights of men." "Property Owning Free African-American Women in the South, 1800–1870," *Journal of Women's History* 1, no. 3 (1990): 24.

111   Eldridge and Whipple, *Memoirs*, 143.

112   Miriam Elizabeth Burstein, "'Unstoried in History'? Early Histories of Women (1652–1902) in the Huntington Library Collections," *The Huntington Library Quarterly* 64, no. 3–4 (2001): 469.

113   Scott E. Casper reports that "Ellet studiously avoided contentious political issues, particularly that of slavery. Occasionally sketches in *The Women of the Revolution* mentioned slaves' presence in southern households, but African-American women were not among Ellet's heroines. Although Ellet lived in Columbia, South Carolina, from about 1835 to 1847, slavery and African Americans appeared infrequently in her

published works, and not at all in her extant letters." "An Uneasy Marriage of Sentiment and Scholarship: Elizabeth F. Ellet and the Domestic Origins of American Women's History," *Journal of Women's History* 4, no. 1 (1992): 31–32n28.

114   Edith B. Gelles, "Review of Casper, Scott E., Constructing American Lives: Biography and Culture in Nineteenth-Century America," H-SHEAR, H-Net Reviews (March 2000): 2, http://www.h-net.org/reviews/showrev.php?id=3938

115   See Lois Brown, "Death-Defying Testimony: Women's Private Lives and the Politics of Public Documents," *Legacy: A Journal of American Women Writers* 27, no. 1 (2010): 130–39.

116   See Jane Lancaster, "A Web of Iniquity? Race, Gender, Foreclosure, and Respectability in Antebellum Rhode Island," *Rhode Island History* 69, no. 2 (2011): 72–92. For Lancaster's detailed discussion of Eldridge's white women patrons (other than Whipple), see especially 74–75.

117   Eldridge and Whipple, *Memoirs,* 97–98.

118   Eldridge and Whipple, *Memoirs,* 149.

119   Eldridge and Whipple, *Memoirs,* 150.

120   Eldridge and Whipple, *Memoirs,* 150n.

121   Eldridge and Whipple, *Memoirs,* 151.

122   Eldridge and Whipple, *Memoirs,* 151–152.

123   Eldridge and Whipple, *Memoirs,* 152.

124   Eldridge and Whipple, *Memoirs,* 153–154. On Catharine Williams's patrilineage, see Rider, *Bibliographical Memoirs,* 51–52; her husband was a sixth-generation descendant from Roger Williams, one of the colonial founders of the state. Moreover, Rider notes that Whipple's *Shahmah in Pursuit of Freedom; or, The Branded Hand* compliments Williams "for her instrumentality in abolishing flogging in the United States navy" (41). Both Whipple and Williams lost their mothers in their youth and were subsequently raised by "maiden aunts." Moreover, the first marriage of each of these two white women authors "proved a most unfortunate one," in Rider's words (52). Both wrote in multiple genres, and each published a history of Fall River. Rider describes Williams as "a warm politician" who "espoused the suffrage party with all her might" (57). Small wonder, then, that she and Whipple were friends and worked together to produce *Memoirs of Elleanor Eldridge.*

125   Eldridge and Whipple, *Memoirs,* 154.

126   Eldridge and Whipple, *Memoirs,* 154–155.

127   Eldridge and Whipple, *Memoirs,* 156–158, 158–163. Later editions of *Memoirs* reversed the order of the final two documents in the appendix, to end with "The Supplication of Elleanor."

128   Eldridge and Whipple, *Memoirs,* 157.

129   Gellman, "Race," 630.

130   Schweninger, "Property Owning," 23.

131   Joanna Brooks, "Our Phillis, Ourselves," *American Literature* 82, no. 1 (2010): 6.

132   Brooks, "Our Phillis," 7.

133   Brooks continues with a sharp critique of Wheatley's white women financial backers, as when she writes: "Their participation in this transactional, sentimental culture of mourning enabled them to indulge feelings of self-consciousness, self-regard, and willful passivity imbricated with their increasingly privileged merchant-class status" ("Our Phillis," 7–8). See "Our Phillis," passim.

134   In his first autobiography, Douglass famously writes of a slave owner who forbade his wife to teach young Douglass the alphabet, "telling her, among other things, that it was unlawful, as well as unsafe, to teach a slave to read. To use his [the slaveholder's] words, further, he said, 'If you give a nigger an inch, he will take an ell.' These words sank deep into my heart, stirred up sentiments within that lay slumbering, and called into existence an entirely new train of thought." *Narrative of the Life of Frederick Douglass, An American Slave*, 1845, in *The Norton Anthology of African American Literature*. 2nd ed., ed. Henry Louis Gates, Jr. and Nellie Y. McKay (New York: W. W. Norton & Co., 2004), 387–452. However, as numerous other scholars (such as Gundaker, "Give Me a Sign," 484) have argued, there is also a record of enslaved people who distrusted print texts because they rightly associated them with the white power structures that maintained the slave trade. Joycelyn Moody, "Silenced Women and Silent Language in Early African- and Anglo-American Newspapers," in *Cultural Narratives: Textuality and Performance in American Culture before 1900*, ed. Sandra Gustafson and Caroline Sloat (Notre Dame: University of Notre Dame Press, 2010), 220–39.

135   Gundaker, "Give Me a Sign," 484.

136   Gundaker, "Give Me a Sign," 484.

137   Gundaker, "Give Me a Sign," 485.

138   Gundaker, "Give Me a Sign," 486.

139   Joanna Brooks, "The Unfortunates: What the Life Spans of Early Black Books Tell Us About Book History," in *Early African American Print Culture*, ed. Lara Langer Cohen and Jordan Alexander Stein (Philadelphia: University of Pennsylvania Press, 2012), 40–52; Eric Gardner, "Remembered (Black) Readers: Subscribers to the *Christian Recorder*, 1864–1865," *American Literary History* 23, no. 2 (2011): 229–59; Frances Smith Foster, "A Narrative of the Interesting Origins and (Somewhat) Surprising Developments of African-American Print Culture," *American Literary History* 17, no. 4 (2005): 714–40; and Frances Smith Foster, "'Looking Back Is Tricky Business . . .'," *Narrative* 18, no. 1 (2010): 19–28.

140   See Gundaker, "Give Me a Sign," 488. Hodges, who reissued The *House Servant's Directory* in 1998 (Robert Roberts and Gore Place Society, *The House Servant's Directory, or, a Monitor for Private Families: Comprising Hints on the Arrangement and Performance of Servants*, ed. Graham Russell Gao Hodges [1827; repr. Armonk, NY: M.E. Sharpe, 1998]) concurs that it is "among the first books written by an African American." Graham Russell Gao Hodges, "Robert Roberts," in *Encyclopedia of African American History, 1619–1895: From the Colonial Period to the Age of Frederick Douglass*, ed. Paul Finkelman (New York: Oxford University Press, 2006), 3:55. I take Roberts's life

dates from Hodges who reports that Roberts cultivated his expertise through domestic service to Boston financier Nathan Appleton (5:54).

141   William Grimes, *Life of William Grimes, the Runaway Slave*, ed. William L. Andrews and Regina E. Mason (1824; repr., New York: Oxford University Press, 2008). *Life of William Grimes* was reprinted in 2008 by William L. Andrews with Grimes's descendant Regina Mason.

142   Gundaker, "Give Me a Sign," 488.

143   Foster, "A Narrative," 716.

144   Foster, "A Narrative," 725–26.

145   Joanna Brooks, "The Early American Public Sphere and the Emergence of a Black Print Counterpublic," *The William and Mary Quarterly* 62, no. 1 (2005): 80.

146   Brooks, "The Early American Public Sphere," 72.

147   Brooks, "The Early American Public Sphere," 75.

148   See Brooks, "The Early American Public Sphere," 68.

149   John C. Crane and Robert Wayland Dunbar, *Centennial History of the Town of Millbury, Massachusetts* (Millbury, 1915), 380. See also http://chroniclingamerica.loc. gov/lccn/sn83020563/ Accessed April 29, 2013.

150   Receipt [for B. T. Albro]. American Antiquarian Society, Brown University, in Thomas Wilson Dorr, Box 2 Folder 22. Access. #A882. Cf. *Printers and Printing in Providence, 1762–1907*, which states that "in 1840 he [Albro] was in business for himself at No. 9 Market square, from which office the first number of the Dorrite paper, the *New Age and Constitutional Advocate*, was issued; in 1844 his office was at No. 2 Canal street; and from 1847 to 1850 at No. 5 Canal street." Providence Typographical Union No. 33, *Printers and Printing in Providence, 1762–1907* (Providence: Providence Print. Co., 1907): III.

151   See, for instance, *The Temperance Annual and Cold Water Magazine* (Baltimore: W. A. Barrett, 1843).

152   Providence Typographical Union, *Printers and Printing*, III.

153   Albro also published *Annals of the Aristocracy* (1845), by C[atharine] R[ead] Williams, who contributed a signed endorsement to the first edition of *Memoirs of Elleanor Eldridge*. C. R. Williams, *Annals of the Aristocracy* (Providence: B. T. Albro, 1845).

154   Frances H. Green [Whipple] and Joseph Whipple Congdon, *Analytical Class-Book of Botany, Designed for Academies and Private Students. In Two Parts* (New York: D. Appleton and Company, 1857). Sidney Smith Rider identifies Whipple as the author of *The Housekeeper's Guide* in *Additions and Corrections to the First Series of Rhode Island Historical Tracts with an Index to the Same. [Rhode Island Historical Tracts. No. 20.]* 1895. *Rhode Island Historical Tracts*, ed. Sidney Smith Rider, vol. 20 (Providence: Snow & Farnham, 1895), 19. Burstein notes that during the Victorian era, many (male and female) writers of women's biographies "also published historical fiction, popular science, etiquette manuals, and the like; Agnes Strickland, the best-known and most-respected among them, began her career as a *bad poet* and later wrote historical fiction, *children's stories*, and book reviews, among other things." "'Unstoried in History'?," 470.

The Library of Congress lists only one *Housekeeper's Guide* published in 1838, and it is neither written by Whipple nor published in the US: Esther Copley, *The Housekeeper's Guide; or, a Plain & Practical System of Domestic Cookery* (London: Longmans & Co., 1838).

155   Marilyn Richardson, "Maria W. Stewart: America's First Black Woman Political Writer," in *Black Women's Intellectual Traditions: Speaking Their Minds*, ed. Kristin Waters and Carol B. Conaway (Lebanon, NH: University Press of New England, 2007), 13.

156   Carol Buchalter Stapp reports that "Black women in antebellum Boston made up 90 percent of the occupational category of domestics, the category accounting for 20 percent of the entire black workforce." *Afro-Americans in Antebellum Boston: An Analysis of Probate Records* (New York: Garland, 1993), 20.

157   David Walker and Peter P. Hinks, *David Walker's Appeal to the Coloured Citizens of the World*, 3rd ed. (1830; repr. University Park: Pennsylvania State University Press, 2000).

158   Richardson, "Maria W. Stewart," 14. See Ampadu for an analysis of ways that Stewart anticipates Alice Walker's womanist theory and other "principles of Africana womanism." Lena Ampadu, "Maria W. Stewart and the Rhetoric of Black Preaching," in *Black Women's Intellectual Traditions: Speaking Their Minds*, ed. Kristin Waters and Carol B. Conaway (Lebanon, NH: University Press of New England, 2007), 41–42.

159   Maria Stewart, *Religion and the Pure Principles of Morality, the Sure Foundation on Which We Must Build* (1831), in *Spiritual Narratives*, ed. Sue E. Houchins (New York: Oxford University Press, 1988).

160   Katherine Clay Bassard, *Transforming Scriptures: African American Women Writers and the Bible* (Athens: University of Georgia Press, 2010), 52. See also Wheelock, "Dividing," 78–80.

161   Stewart, "Religion," 16. Gundaker speculates that, earlier, "in 1827, writing to *Freedom's Journal*, an individual who signed her name 'Matilda' was perhaps the first African American woman to submit a letter to an editor." Urging women's rights, Matilda opposed "too much cooking and too little reading in the education of females." "Give Me a Sign," 488. Matilda also wrote "On Reading the Poems of Phillis Wheatley, the African Poetess" (in *New-York Magazine*, October 1796, 549–50). Later, Margaretta Matilda Odell published *Memoir and Poems of Phillis Wheatley, a Native African and a Slave* (Boston: Geo. W. Light, 1834).

162   Stewart, "Religion," 78.

163   Richardson, "Maria W. Stewart," 16.

164   Ampadu, "Maria W. Stewart," 40.

165   Eileen Boris, "From Gender to Racialized Gender: Laboring Bodies That Matter," *International Labor and Working-Class History* 63 (2003): 10–11.

166   Ebony A. Utley, "A Woman Made of Words: The Rhetorical Invention of Maria W. Stewart," in *Black Women's Intellectual Traditions: Speaking Their Minds*, ed.

Kristin Waters and Carol B. Conaway (Lebanon, NH: University Press of New England, 2007), 59.

167   See Kathy L. Glass on Stewart's cultivation and endorsement of bourgeois values in *Courting Communities: Black Female Nationalism and "Syncre-Nationalism" in the Nineteenth-Century North* (New York: Routledge, 2006).

168   Stewart would repeat this rhetorical gesture in her second publication, *Meditations from the Pen of Mrs. Maria W. Stewart* (Washington, 1879).

169   The portrait of Eldridge contrasts sharply with Joseph T. Zealy's infamous daguerreotypes of enslaved women commissioned over a decade later by Louis Agassiz. See Brian Wallis, "Black Bodies, White Science: Louis Agassiz's Slave Daguerreotypes," *American Art* 9, no. 2 (Summer 1995): 39–61.

170   Charles Johnson, "The Transmission," *Soulcatcher and Other Stories* (San Diego: Harcourt, 2001), 1–11.

171   Andrews, *To Tell*, 39.

172   Foster, "Looking Back Is Tricky Business," 20.

173   Julia Winch's recovery of *The Elite of Our People* (originally published in 1841 by Joseph Wilson) provides excellent information about 19th-century US black people's complex attitudes about wealth, money, and social and class status. See Winch, ed., *The Elite of Our People: Joseph Willson's Sketches of Black Upper-Class Life in Antebellum Philadelphia*. University Park: Pennsylvania State University Press, 2000. Print.

174   Joanne Pope Melish gives Chloe Prophet's birth year as 1744, the same year that *Memoirs* gives as Hannah's birth year. Although there is no evidence that Chloe and Hannah were twins, it is possible that both were born to Mary Fuller. More likely, however, Chloe Prophet's birth date is misprinted in Melish's introduction and should be given as 1644, in which case, Chloe could have given birth to Mary Fuller in 1678. Melish, introduction, xvi, xxi–xxii.

175   *Births, Marriages, Deaths,* City [of Providence, RI] Archives, accessed April 5, 2011, in the City Archives, Providence City Hall, 25 Dorrance Street, Providence, Rhode Island 02903. The death record names her as *"Ellen,* d[aughter] of Robert, (col'd), 76 years" (italics added). The Ellenor Eldridge cited in the 1870 census is listed as a white woman eighty-one years old and living in Warwick.

176   Quigley and Finkelman, "Rhode Island," 41.

177   Eldridge and Whipple, *Memoirs,* 103–104. Rhode Island collected its first census in 1790. I could find no data on Mary Fuller.

178   On Narragansett women's purchases of enslaved black men, see Melish, introduction, xx. Melish also discusses the confusion about descendants of the Prophet line that emerges in *The Life of William J. Brown of Providence, R. I.* As Melish notes, Brown seems to have been a relative of Eldridge's, given the commonality of names in their life stories (xvi, xxi xxii). The 1860 Rhode Island census records one possible descendant of Mary and Thomas's union: Thomas Prophet, a Black male forty years old, living in Warwick. Ten years later, he is recorded as the forty-six-year-old head of a

household of four persons living in Providence County, where he works as a coachman. http://persi.heritagequestonline.com.libweb.lib.utsa.edu/hqoweb/library/do/census/search/basic

179   The Eldridges named *Elenor*, *George*, and *Settes*—none of whom are identified as white —appear for the first time in the Rhode Island census in 1820. They are recorded as living in Warwick (Kent County), Rhode Island. A Jemima Eldridge, living in Smithfield (Providence County), Rhode Island, is listed as living alone; her racial identity is not designated. The same categorization as Jemima pertains to a Rachel Eldridge. According to HeritageQuest Online (last consulted July 7, 2011), by 1860 forty-six Eldridges were counted in the census. Three of these are designated as black and living in Providence County: Ellen (age 76; presumably the subject of *Memoirs of Elleanor Eldridge*), Mary (age 20), and Samuel H. (age 28). Two adult nonwhite Eldridge males are identified as M[ulatto] in the 1860 Warwick, Rhode Island, census: George R. (age 38) and Robert M. (age 50); also listed as "mulatto" in the same place are Sarah (age 32) and Emily (age 36), women who seem to be the respective spouses of George and Robert and mothers of the six "mulatto" children also named Eldridge and living in either Robert's household or George's. Ten years later, the 1870 census names only thirty-seven Eldridges; more of these persons are identified as black or mulatto. Notably, of the three Samuels listed in the 1870 census (and born in Rhode Island), none are identified as black or mulatto. However, the Samuel whose age is given as thirty-three in 1870 might well refer to Samuel H. Eldridge, identified in the 1860 census as black and aged twenty-eight (and born in Connecticut), and perhaps Elleanor Eldridge's younger relation. That Eldridge's kin, in the custom of the era, named children for parents and other kin is clear in Eldridge's death record. On the same page, for example, we find death records for Caroline Eldridge, "d[aughter] of Geo. R., (col'd), 13 yrs."; John A. Eldridge, s[on] of John (col'd), 5 yrs; Philip H., s[on] of Geo. R., (col'd), 3 yrs." http://persi.heritagequestonline.com.libweb.lib.utsa.edu/hqoweb/library/do/census/search/basic. With respect to repeated family names, Fulton references Mary Helen Washington's comments on this practice in a discussion of Sojourner Truth: "That Truth named at least four of her children after her parents and siblings [illustrates] how through oral traditions Truth recreated her family and expressed their identities." Fulton continues, "In contrast to theories suggesting the obliteration of identity through forced separation during slavery, Truth's naming practices represent an oral resistance to the physical destruction of familial relationships caused by slavery." *Speaking Power*, 5.

180   Eldridge and Whipple, *Memoirs*, 103.

181   Eldridge and Whipple, *Memoirs*, 104.

182   Eldridge and Whipple, *Memoirs*, 104. For a definition of orphan, see *American Heritage® Dictionary of the English Language*, 4th ed., 2000.

183   Eldridge and Whipple, *Memoirs*, 104.

184   Herndon and Sekatau, "The Right to a Name," 438.

185   John E. Murray and Ruth Wallis Herndon, "Markets for Children in Early

America: A Political Economy of Pauper Apprenticeship," *Journal of Economic History* 62, no. 2 (2002): 356–82, 359, 365, and 370. Murray and Herndon note that "Rhode Island indentures bound a disproportionate number of children of color. A quarter of all children were black or Indian (or mulatto or mustee or other variation), while only six percent of Rhode Islanders in the 1790 census were nonwhite" (370). Also see Ruth Wallis Herndon on eighteenth century Rhode Island's Native American poor people, in which Herndon analyzes Rhode Island's population with respect to gender, race, region, and caste to discuss poor relief and indenture arrangements for poor children of color. "'Who Died an Expense to This Town,'" in *Down and Out in Early America*, ed. Billy G. Smith (University Park: Pennsylvania State University Press, 2004), 135–62.

186   David J. Silverman, "The Impact of Indentured Servitude on the Society and Culture of Southern New England Indians, 1680–1810," *New England Quarterly* 74, no. 4 (2001): 622–666, 623.

187   Herndon and Sekatau, "The Right to a Name," 441.

188   Murray and Herndon, "Markets for Children," 369.

189   Murray and Herndon, "Markets for Children," 372, 376.

190   Gundaker, "Give Me a Sign," 484.

191   Eldridge and Whipple, *Memoirs*, 97.

192   See Murray and Herndon for more on craft apprenticeships in Rhode Island ("Markets for Children," *passim*).

193   Thank you to an anonymous West Virginia University Press reviewer for this insight.

194   Eldridge and Whipple, *Memoirs*, 116. According to *Memoirs*, a Probate Court had granted Eldridge's sister Lettise custody of their younger siblings (62). Finkelman reports that Eldridge had six sisters. Paul Finkelman, "Elleanor Eldridge," in *Encyclopedia of African American History, 1619–1895: From the Colonial Period to the Age of Frederick Douglass*, ed. Paul Finkelman (New York: Oxford University Press, 2006), 1:457.

195   Compare Stapp, who comments on black women workers in other urban centers in antebellum New England: "in antebellum Philadelphia, 80 percent of the black female workforce did daywork, 14 were seamstresses, and 5 percent were vending cart proprietors. . . . In short, the vast preponderance of black workers carried out unskilled or semiskilled jobs, with very little differentiation in occupation." *Afro-Americans*, 20.

196   James Oliver Horton and Lois E. Horton, *In Hope of Liberty: Culture, Community, and Protest among Northern Free Blacks, 1700–1860* (New York: Oxford University Press, 1997), 116.

197   Joanne Pope Melish, "Workers and Whiteness Revisited," *Labor: Studies in Working-Class History of the Americas* 5, no. 4 (2008): 66. Eric Gardner discusses the complications of assigning class categories to antebellum African Americans; he persuasively concludes that "occupation should only be one variable in a complex equation toward identifying class status" for blacks. "Remembered (Black) Readers: Subscribers

to the *Christian Recorder*, 1864–1865," *American Literary History* 23, no. 2 (2011): 28n33. See also scholarship on "the black middle class" in Edward Franklin Frazier, *Black Bourgeoisie* (Glencoe, IL: Free Press, 1957); Lawrence Graham, *Our Kind of People: Inside America's Black Upper Class* (New York: HarperCollins, 1999); Vershawn Ashanti Young and Bridget Harris Tsemo, eds., *From Bourgeois to Boojie: Black Middle-Class Performances* (Detroit: Wayne State University Press, 2011); David R. Roediger, *Towards the Abolition of Whiteness: Essays on Race, Politics, and Working Class History*, The Haymarket Series (New York: Verso, 1994); David R. Roediger, *The Wages of Whiteness: Race and the Making of the American Working Class*, rev. ed. (New York: Verso, 2007); and William J. Wilson, *More Than Just Race: Being Black and Poor in the Inner City* (New York: Norton & Company, 2009).

198   For this discussion, I rely on Frances Smith Foster and Claudia May, "Class," in *The Oxford Companion to African American Literature*, ed. William L. Andrews, Frances Smith Foster, and Trudier Harris (New York: Oxford University Press, 1997), 153–56.

199   Quoted in Farah Jasmine Griffin, ed., *Beloved Sisters and Loving Friends* (New York: Ballantine, 2001), 28. See Griffin on the fluid, often precarious middle-class status of the Primuses, an African American family in nineteenth-century Hartford, Connecticut.

200   Eldridge and Whipple, *Memoirs*, 33. On black elections involving free, but disenfranchised, black men in Warwick, see Joseph P. Reidy, "Negro Election Day and Black Community Life in New England, 1750–1860," *Marxist Perspectives* 1 (1978): 102–17; Melvin Wade, "'Shining in Borrowed Plumage': Affirmation of Community in the Black Coronation Festivals of New England (c. 1750–c. 1850)," *Western Folklore* 40, no. 3 (1981): 211–31; and Shane White, "'It Was a Proud Day': African Americans, Festivals, and Parades in the North, 1741–1834," *The Journal of American History* 81, no. 1 (1994): 13–50. The election system in part (though very complicated and sometimes used to reify minstrelsy) attests to the choice made by free blacks like (and perhaps including) Elleanor Eldridge and her brother to rebut the racialized hiring discrimination they suffered. That is, they earned their livelihoods through physical labor, sometimes unskilled labor or labor far beneath their capabilities. This work was at odds with the social prestige and socioeconomic status they apparently enjoyed among other people of color in Providence. Though a proprietor, as a woman, Elleanor would not have been able to vote in the election that yielded her brother's governorship, even though she was successfully self-employed and also owned more property than many of the men who voted in that election. William J. Brown gives a sardonic account of black elections. *The Life of William J. Brown of Providence, R.I.: With Personal Recollections of Incidents in Rhode Island*, ed. Rosalind Cobb Wiggins and Joanne Pope Melish (Durham: University of New Hampshire Press, 2006), 56. Jane Lancaster reports that the duties of the negro governor included mediation between Rhode Island's black population and white civil authorities. "Elleanor Eldridge," in *The Encyclopedia of New England*, ed. Burt Feintuch

and David H. Watts (New Haven: Yale University Press, 2005), 362–63. See Lancaster, "A Web of Iniquity?" (78–79), for a richly detailed discussion of George's election and service as African governor of Warwick.

201   Eldridge and Whipple, *Memoirs*, 119.

202   Foster, "Gender, Genre and Vulgar Secularism: The Case of Frances Ellen Watkins Harper and the AME Press," in *Recovered Writers/ Recovered Texts: Race, Class, and Gender in Black Women's Literature*, ed. Dolan Hubbard (Knoxville: University of Tennessee Press, 1997), 46–59, 58n11.

203   Among numerous black feminist scholarly analyses of Baartman's life and captivity, see Janell Hobson, *Venus in the Dark: Blackness and Beauty in Popular Culture* (New York: Routledge, 2005) and T. Denean Sharpley-Whiting, *Black Venus: Sexualized Savages, Primal Fears, and Primitive Narratives in French* (Durham: Duke University Press 1999).

204   Augusta Rohrbach, *Truth Stranger Than Fiction: Race, Realism, and the U.S. Literary Marketplace* (New York: Palgrave, 2002).

205   Michael A. Chaney, *Fugitive Vision: Slave Image and Black Identity in Antebellum Narrative* (Bloomington: Indiana University Press, 2008).

206   For more on African and African American author frontispiece portraits, see, e.g., Lynn A. Casmier-Paz, "Slave Narratives and the Rhetoric of Author Portraiture," *New Literary History* 34, no. 1 (2003): 91–116, and Barbara E. Lacey, "Visual Images of Blacks in Early American Imprints," *William and Mary Quarterly* 53, no. 1 (1996): 137–80.

207   Xiomara Santamarina, *Belabored Professions: Narratives of African American Working Womanhood* (Chapel Hill: University of North Carolina Press, 2005). Notably, there is no mention of Eldridge or her portrait in Nell Irvin Painter's *Creating Black Americans: African-American History and Its Meanings, 1619 to the Present* (New York: Oxford University Press, 2006), a history of African Americans that emphasizes black art and creativity, perhaps because the artist is unknown.

208   Alan Trachtenberg, *Reading American Photographs: Images as History, Mathew Brady to Walker Evans* (New York: Hill and Wang, 1989). See especially 240–41.

209   See Trachtenberg, 26, 29.

210   On images of people of African descent from the seventeenth century to the present, see Deborah Willis and Carla Williams, eds., *The Black Female Body: A Photographic History* (Philadelphia: Temple University Press, 2002).

211   Lancaster, "Web," gives the population of Providence in 1820 as 11,767, and the number of free blacks in the city in 1815 as 865 (90n22, 76–7).

212   On inking people of color in nineteenth-century print texts, see Jonathan Senchyne, "'Bottles of Ink, and Reams of Paper': Clotel, Racialization, and the Material Culture of Print," in *Early African American Print Culture in Theory and Practice*, ed. Lara Langer Cohen and Jordan Alexander Stein (Philadelphia: University of Pennsylvania Press), 140–58.

213   Cf. William J. Brown's documentation of his repeated wrangling with white employers to receive the full amount of pay negotiated for his services (*The Life of William J. Brown*). For the dangers faced by free(d) and enslaved women of color with respect to labor and employment, see also Tera W. Hunter, *To 'Joy My Freedom: Southern Black Women's Lives and Labors after the Civil War* (Cambridge: Harvard University Press, 1997); Jacqueline Jones, *Labor of Love, Labor of Sorrow: Black Women, Work and the Family, from Slavery to the Present*, 4th ed. (New York: Basic Books, 2010); and Deborah G. White, *Ar'n't I a Woman?: Female Slaves in the Plantation South*, rev. ed. (New York: W.W. Norton, 1999). For the specific case of Addie Brown as a skilled, working-class black woman in mid-nineteenth-century Connecticut, see Karen V. Hansen, "'No Kisses Is Like Youres': An Erotic Friendship between Two African-American Women During the Mid-Nineteenth Century," *Gender and History* 7, no. 2 (1995): 153–82; and Farah Jasmine Griffin, ed., *Beloved Sisters and Loving Friends* (New York, NY: Ballantine, 2001).

214   Jeffrey L. Pasley, "The Cheese and the Words: Popular Political Culture and Participatory Democracy in the Early American Republic," in Jeffrey L. Pasley, Andrew W. Robertson, and David Waldstreicher, eds., *Beyond the Founders: New Approaches to the Political History of the Early American Republic* (Chapel Hill: University of North Carolina Press, 2004), 31–56. I am grateful to the West Virginia University Press reviewer who referred me to the collection of essays by Pasley et al.

215   Louis Masur, "'Pictures Have Now Become a Necessity': The Use of Images in American History Textbooks," *Journal of American History* 84, no. 4(1998): 1409–23.

216   Chaney, 29.

217   Robert Roberts, *The House Servant's Directory, or, a Monitor for Private Families: Comprising Hints on the Arrangement and Performance of Servants' Work . . . And Upwards of 100 Various and Useful Receipts. Chiefly Compiled for the Use of House Servants* (Boston: Munroe and Francis, C. S. Francis, 1827).

218   Hodges, "Robert Roberts," 55. Hodges references Roberts's purchase of his family home in "Introduction," *The House Servant's Directory*, by Robert Roberts (Armonk, NY: Sharpe, 1998), xix.

219   Brown tells two stories of his African-descended family's having been swindled out of Rhode Island real estate by Moses Brown of Providence and other elite whites (*Life of William J. Brown*, 9, 14, 16, 125–36).

220   O'Dowd, *A Rhode Island Original*, 22–23.

221   David Walker, *Appeal to the Coloured Citizens of the World*, 11–12.

222   Eldridge and Whipple, *Elleanor's Second Book*, 27.

223   See Lancaster, "A Web of Iniquity?," *passim*, for a detailed discussion of the "numerous inconsistencies between the *Memoirs* and existing documentary evidence" (72).

224   I am very grateful to colleagues who helped me articulate the complexities of the impact of Eldridge's court cases.

225   Blevins, "'Owned by Negro Venture,'" 130; emphasis added.

226   Ruth Wallis Herndon and Ella Wilcox Sekatau, "The Right to a Name: The Narragansett People and Rhode Island Officials in the Revolutionary Era," *Ethnohistory* 44, no. 3 (1997): 438.

227   Census records for Rhode Island in 1810 include a Benjamin Greene as well as a Benjamin Greene II, both of Johnston County. See also O'Dowd, 22 and Lancaster, 80.

228   Eldridge and Whipple, *Memoirs*, 127.

229   Eldridge and Whipple, *Memoirs*, 128. Lancaster identifies this sister as Sallie Eldridge. See "Web of Iniquity?," 80.

230   A May 18, 1826, receipt for Eldridge asserts that she had purchased land on May 28, 1820.

231   Silverman, "The Impact," 633.

232   Rhode Island and Providence Plantations Supreme Court Judicial Records, May 1826 (State of Rhode Island and Providence Plantations Supreme Court Judicial Records Center, Pawtucket, RI). For further analysis of the legal cases in which Eldridge was involved, see Jennifer D. Brody and Sharon P. Holland, "An/ Other Case of New England Underwriting: Negotiating Race and Property in Memoirs of Elleanor Eldridge," in *Crossing Waters, Crossing Worlds: The African Diaspora in Indian Country*, ed. Tiya Miles and Sharon P. Holland (Durham, NC: Duke University Press, 2006), 31–56. Detailed analyses of Eldridge's purchasing history and the extant records of her real estate acquisitions and the disputes they occasioned is the focus of Lancaster, "A Web of Iniquity?."

233   Rhode Island and Providence Plantations Supreme Court Judicial Records, May 1826.

234   Eldridge and Whipple, *Memoirs*, 128. See also Lancaster, "Web," 82.

235   Lancaster argues that this second episode of typhus decommissioned Eldridge and rendered her unable to work and thus unable to repay her loan ("Web," 84).

236   See Eldridge and Whipple, *Memoirs*, 131.

237   See Lancaster, "A Web of Iniquity?," 81–88.

238   Rhode Island and Providence Plantations Supreme Court Judicial Records, February 1834.

239   Quigley and Finkelman, "Rhode Island," 42. Quigley and Finkelman continue, "By 1860, they held over $61,600 worth of real estate and personal property valued at more than $10,600" (42). Rhode Island tax records list Eldridge as still paying taxes in 1860.

240   John Carder v. Elenor [*sic*] Eldridge, Court of Common Pleas, January 20, 1835.

241   Eldridge and Whipple, *Memoirs*, 104. *Memoirs of Elleanor Eldridge* states that "this case was brought before the Court of Common Pleas, in January, 1837" (141); however, documents forwarded to the author from Rhode Island courts in February 2011 do not include record of a trespass suit Eldridge filed against Balch.

242 John Carder v. Elleanor Eldridge. On mid-nineteenth-century US obsession with personal character, see Karen Halttunen, *Confidence Men and Painted Women: A Study of Middle-Class Culture in America, 1830–1870* (New Haven: Yale University Press, 1982).

243 The text of John Carder v. Elenor [sic] Eldridge (Court of Common Pleas, January 20, 1835) constitutes a warrant for Eldridge's arrest.

244 Herndon and Sekatau, "The Right to a Name," 441.

245 Herndon and Sekatau, "The Right to a Name," 449.

246 Herndon and Sekatau, "The Right to a Name," 451.

247 Herndon and Sekatau, "The Right to a Name," 451.

248 Rider, *Bibliographical Memoirs*, 36.

249 Rider, *Bibliographical Memoirs*, 37. Catharine R. Williams, one of Eldridge's inscribed supporters, was the granddaughter of mid-eighteenth-century Rhode Island Attorney General Oliver Arnold. Perhaps Williams's relational tie gave Eldridge access to the RI Attorney General in the early 1830s.

250 Ellenor Eldredge v. Benjamin Balch, Providence [RI] Court of Common Pleas, May [Term] 1836.

251 Lancaster, "Web," 86.

252 Ellenor Eldredge v. Benjamin Balch.

253 A warrant to arrest Balch to answer a legal complaint from Eldridge was filed in Court of Common Pleas, Providence, Rhode Island, on May 2, 1836. A Providence Schedule dated Feb 1, 1837, recorded the mandate of court appearances by Ben Lockwood, Henry Martin, Elleanor Eldridge, and Benjamin Balch "on the fourth Monday of Nov A.D. 1836 to give evidence of what you know relating to an action of Trespass & Ejectment then and there to be heard between Eleanor Eldridge Plaintiff and Benjamin Belch Defendant." "Providence sc. The State of Rhode-Island and Providence Plantations," Providence May 2nd 1836.

254 *List of Persons Assessed in the City Tax . . . ordered by the City Council, June 1836* (Providence: H. H. Brown, 1836).

255 The edition of the *List of Persons Assessed in the City Tax . . . ordered by the City Council on March 13, 1848*, is missing pages 28–33, so it is undetermined whether Eldridge paid taxes that year.

256 Numerous social historians focused on gender and women have addressed this matter; see, for example, Herndon and Sekatau, "The Right to a Name."

257 See Jeannine Marie DeLombard, *Slavery on Trial: Law, Abolitionism, and Print Culture* (Chapel Hill: University of North Carolina Press, 2007).

258 Eldridge and Whipple, *Memoirs*, 93.

259 See Christina Accomando, *The Regulations of Robbers: Legal Fictions of Slavery and Resistance* (Columbus: The Ohio State University Press, 2001); and also Nell Irvin Painter, *Sojourner Truth: A Life, a Symbol* (New York: Norton, 1996).

260 Humez, "Reading," 32.

261   See Humez, "Reading," 32n55. On the reparations petition of Belinda Isaac, see Sharon M. Harris, "Belinda: The Politics of Petitions," in her *Executing Race: Early American Women's Narratives of Race, Society, and the Law* (Columbus: Ohio State University Press, 2005).

262   Humez, "Reading," 32.

263   *Memoirs* includes an episode highlighting Eldridge's negotiations with Rhode Island courts that included her brother George's involvements with law enforcement. In April 1832, George Eldridge "was, for an alleged crime, arrested and thrown into prison. He was accused of having horse-whipped, and of otherwise barbarously treating a man upon the highway"; Elleanor went to his rescue, against the caution of "her friends," as she purportedly chose rather to obey "alone the dictates of humanity, benevolence, and natural love, [and] she generously committed herself to the guardianship of her brother's rights" (97–98). Eldridge applied her property to George's trial, which was twice delayed before his ultimate acquittal. According to *Memoirs*, "Elleanor managed this case entirely; and, on account of it, was subjected to considerable cost and trouble; but she never regretted having engaged in it, and would freely have expended much more, had it been necessary to effect her purpose" (99). A clear rhetorical aim of the episode is to emphasize Eldridge's perseverance and skill, to show her a match for men if a fight were fair.

264   Rohrbach, 40. See *Valuation of Taxable Property, in the Town of Warwick, as apportioned by the assessors of taxes, February 7th, A.D. 1856* (Providence: Sayles, Miller, and Simons, 1856). *List of Persons and Corporations who were Assessed in the City Tax . . . Ordered by the City Council of Providence for the Year 1856* (Providence: H. H. Brown, 1856).

265   Lancaster, "Web," 73.

266   Rider, *Bibliographical Memoirs*, 37.

267   A death record in *Births, Marriages, Deaths*, City [of Providence, RI] Archives identifies one "*Ellen*, d[aughter] of Robert, (col'd), 76 years" (italics added). The *Ellenor* Eldridge cited in the 1870 census is listed as a white woman eighty-one years old and living in Warwick. The *List of Persons and Corporations Who Are Assessed in . . . Warwick . . . 1865* includes an *Ellen Eldridge* of East Greenwich, Rhode Island, as paying $1,200 in taxes on real estate property worth $20,000.

A Final Note on Recovering
Memoirs of Elleanor Eldridge:
plus les choses changent . . .

My sister, have you got your sword and shield. . . .
I got 'em fo' I left the field[.]

—Anonymous, "Marching Up the Heavenly Road"[1]

We confess to their views as objectionable, as we know them to be, but this does not close our eyes against the 'humbug' connected with this abolition reform, some phases of which would cause a worm-eating New Hollander to hide his head from very disgust.

—Mary Ann Shadd Cary, "The Humbug of Reform"[2]

It is important that they should, as an undying incentive to energy and perseverance, be inspired with the conviction that the finger of God is pointing them to that land—that they have a great mission to fulfill there—that the strong hand of Providence is stretched out to bring them to their promised land—that the land is kept in reserve, waiting for its rightful occupants.

—Hollis Read, *The Negro Problem Solved,
or, Africa as She Was, as She Is, and as She Shall Be;
Her Curse and Her Cure*[3]

Recovering and reissuing life narratives by people of color of the colonial and early national periods of the United States poses significant challenges to twenty-first literary historians, despite digitization and other technological advancements. When white Americans were involved in the recording, printing, and publishing of those early narratives, as they almost always were, in and around the life stories one may find abundant evidence that exposes the racial minefields through which the minoritized authors gingerly made their way into print. Recovery work, then, is difficult when the life reconstructed is that of an 1830's woman of African and indigenous descent, and the scholar who would reissue her life narrative is a black woman working within and against an unseeing white power structure over two centuries old. If the narrative is to get into twenty-first-century readers' hands, both the black woman of the past and her contemporary counterpart must carefully circumvent whites' fantasies of black women: namely, those harmful stereotypes and controlling images, to invoke Patricia Hill Collins's punning phrase, of angry, violent antagonists.[4] Perhaps the greatest challenge for recovery work by, of, and about US black women manifests when the subjects of the recovery project and the scholars involved are themselves African American women because so few white people with publishing power abjure changing the nature of the relationships that accord them power or interrogating the bases of their fantasies of black women's alleged, mythic power over them.

Writing about *Memoirs of Elleanor Eldridge*, Jane Lancaster significantly titles her *Rhode Island History* essay "A Web of Iniquity? Race, Gender, Foreclosure, and *Respectability* in Antebellum Rhode Island" (italics added). For Lancaster, it is Eldridge who grapples with *race, gender, foreclosure* problems, and *respectability*. She illustrates the "respectability" of her title in one instance by quoting Whipple's insistence that "Elleanor has always lived with good people," and further noting Whipple's emphasis on "Eldridge's respectability and good connections."[5] Also, Lancaster quotes one of Whipple's rare attributions of Eldridge's direct speech: "'I went to Boston and found a great many kind friends there, very kind indeed,' she told Whipple. She was certainly in contact with the abolitionist *Liberator*, in whose Boston offices the book was available. "'There I sold about three hundred books; and they furnished me with letters to the most respectable colored people, and other friends in New York'" (Lancaster, "Web of Iniquity," 43). Notably, what Evelyn Brooks Higginbotham theorized in 1992 as African American women's "politics of respectability" not only determined the directions of black political activism and protest against racial inequality at the Jim Crow turn into the twentieth century,[6] but Higginbotham's term named (names) a code of respectability, a signification of double consciousness judiciously cohering in numerous African American texts in which white editors and publishers are involved, even by black authors labeled—some zealously touted—"militant" or "confrontational."[7]

Sometimes not even death protects a black woman author from "white-washing" when a white publisher is involved in the printing of her text, no matter the public persona she fashions for herself, as Lois Brown demonstrates in "Memorial Narratives of African Women in Antebellum New England." Brown observes that for the obituary of Africa-born poet Lucy Terry Prince (1724–1821) printed in the August 1, 1821, issue, the *Vermont Gazette* "use[d] white church and town records as its primary sources," rather than resources, including memories and retentions, from the African community and black ethnic contexts in which Prince was deeply rooted. The documents from white institutions emphasize such 'civilizing' aspects of Prince's life "as her first church affiliations, her [Christian] baptism, and the legal details surrounding the family's acquisition of land and their fight to protect the boundaries of that property in Northfield, Vermont."[8] Brown concludes that as "these details confer a measure of civic respectability on Prince, they also represent an insidious whitewashing of black history, an attempt to 'efface the indigenous experience of slavery,'" and she rightly suggests "that effacement [was] prompted by [whites'] disregard, shame, or miseducation" ("Memorial Narrataives," 43). Although Lucy Terry Prince remains one of the most anthologized and (thus) best known women poets in the colonial United States, in fact, the version, the controlled and controlling image, of Prince's life circulating since 1821 is in part a fantasy of African womanhood devised by white editors. For Prince's print legacy, they settled on iconic black womanhood honorable and benign, peaceful and Christian—an especially ironic choice considering that Prince's most acclaimed poem narrates an account of a raid by indigenous people on white settlers in Deerfield, Vermont, that is, a *race war*.

Seventeen years later, Frances Whipple would not depict Elleanor Eldridge as a Christian; however, what Whipple does with Eldridge parallels the actions and choices of white editors who commemorated Prince: she imagines and removes the elements of Africanity and indigeneity that—in whatever way—putatively threaten Whipple herself and that compel her to project the alien traits as potential dangers imposed on (white) readers of Eldridge's *Memoirs*. Yet, as I demonstrate throughout this Introduction, Whipple aligns herself and other white women with Eldridge, as also victims of sex, gender, and class oppression—even when she charges passionately that had Eldridge been a white woman she would have been treated more humanely, more justly than she was.[9] Significantly, though, Whipple does not recognize her privileges of whiteness and womanness, nor her own oppressive capabilities and performances. Eldridge's work is all the harder, then, if the biography is to be published and printed and to bring her the resources she needs to fund her lawsuits and regain her property. In 1838, despite a flourishing black press 100 miles away in Boston, Eldridge's clear choices are to access Providence's (white) print culture by means of signfying and a politics-of-respectability dance with her white coauthor and their white printer, or to do without biography, mortgage, land, and paradoxically, self-reliance.

If Eldridge did not want to suffer in life the ethnic and cultural obliteration to which Lucy Terry Prince had been subjected after death, she had few rhetorical options. One choice Eldridge wisely avoided was that made by Sylvia Dubois (1768?–1888),[10] eponymous angry and violent black woman icon at the center of *Sylvia Dubois, (Now 116 Years Old.) a Biografy of the Slav Who Whipt Her Mistres and Gand Her Fredom*, by C[ornelius] W[ilson] Larison, M. D., in 1883. Later, in 1888, as represented in an obituary incongruously titled "A Famous Negress," Dubois cuts a less palatable, more familiar fiction of black womanhood, embodying white fears of African barbarity unbound.[11] In "'The Peals of Her Terrific Language': The Control of Representation in 'Silvia Dubois, a Biografy of the Slav Who Whipt Her Mistres and Gand Her Fredom,'" Michael C. Berthold underscores the code of female respectability consciously at play in a regional obituary of Dubois published in 1888. Reflecting on such qualities the obituary attributes to Dubois as her legendary "'fondness for fighting, for liquor, and her profanity,'" Berthold writes: "In this folkloric résumé paragraph of might and gigantism, Dubois spurns her culture's tyrannies of decorum, station, and *femininity.* Her transgender combat and independent maternity reject male prerogative and protection; her very public notoriety (her fighting, drinking, and vernacular outspokenness) overturns both the expected obeisance of the 'good' slave and the genteel anonymity of the *'true' woman.* As carnal centenarian, Dubois seems to defy temporality itself" ("Peals of Her Terrific Language," 3).

The consequences of such a discursive choice—congruent with public adaptation to the controlling image of black female carnality— would have been acute for Elleanor Eldridge, though a measure of economic autonomy in early nineteenth-century Rhode Island might well have remained open to her. For Dubois was a second-generation black property owner on Sourland Mountain, New Jersey, having inherited from her maternal grandfather an ill-reputed, unlicensed tavern known as "Put's Old House" (Fulton Minor and Pitts, *Speaking Lives,* 25). Homeownership, motherwit, and chutzpah kept Sylvia Dubois in trouble and dispute with local law enforcement and tax assessors until, in 1841, the tavern was mysteriously burned and she was left destitute—one penalty exacted of her as a "loud," "unruly" black women exerting bravery and independence. Had Eldridge not comported herself in ways designed to steer white women into perceiving her as a compliant, controllable "colored" woman, then her hopes for real estate ownership and entrepreneurship would certainly have been compromised to say the least. Thus, burdened with white power's controlling image of the angry, aggressive black woman, Eldridge—born free just one year into Rhode Island's emancipation act—would likely have had no mortgages, no land, no lawsuits, no presence in the Providence tax records, and most significant of all, perhaps no relationship with Frances Whipple and no *Memoirs.* After all, very few recent standard encyclopedias and reference biographies of African Americans include mention of Sylvia Dubois; to most she remains altogether unknown.[12] Rather, far more common for black and/or indigenous women such as Eldridge has been an utter lack of documentation of their lives at all, with the possible exception of a death notice, and in the case of the putative bad black woman, even in death, a defamatory remembrance.[13]

As it is, to recover a life (and) narrative such as Eldridge's, first finding, then restructuring the extant bits and shards in the shattered historical, "official" record demands abundant resources, among them care, hope, help, time, luck, and faith. Moreover, in the case of the African American woman scholar who would restore *Memoirs of Elleanor Eldridge* for contemporary readers, patience, too, is required to endure and assuage the inevitable anxieties of white editors and publishers who see in "race" a black bogeyman and thus do "not deal with race as a cultural, environmental, economic, political, theological, regional, or legal construction and subsequent process."[14] When the life-writing subject is a woman with book learning and formal literacy skills such as Harriet Jacobs, the labor of reconstructing her life and times is only marginally easier. Jean Fagan Yellin acknowledges in the prefatory texts of *The Harriet Jacobs Family Papers* that the creation of that vast collection took three decades—*thirty years*—and the involvement of "multitudes."[15] Jacobs's racial classification as "mulatto" during her lifetime perhaps was not irrelevant in this case. One imagines whiteness—Child's, Yellin's, Jacobs's own—playing a felicitous role, however, and Yellin encountering little resistance as she published her two-volume reference compilation within an editorial model that replicated nineteenth-century ones. By contrast, Jacobs's complicated relationships with nineteenth-century white authors Lydia Maria Child, Amy Post, and Harriet Beecher Stowe are well documented.[16]

Indeed, an ironic redundancy reverberates in black feminist scholarly recovery of early national black women's life narratives, in ways akin to those of the Mandelbrot set that functions for John Ernest as a trope in his book *Chaotic Justice: Rethinking African American Literary History*. Thinking through crucial difficulties and necessities that African Americanist literary historians must confront in the twenty-first century, Ernest uses this figure to describe in particular William Still's narrative mode of history-making in *The Underground Rail Road: A Record of Facts, Authentic Narratives, Letters, &c.* (1872) as well as the "fluid" and "dynamic" nature of African American literary history making more broadly defined (*Chaotic Justice*, 214). Ernest cogently reads Still's text as in effect "a book of fragments, often gesturing to the many stories that could be constructed from those fragments, woven together to tell a story whose suggested contours press against the available contexts for understanding its scope and significance" (*Chaotic Justice*, 214). A Mandelbrot set intrigues for its repetition in miniature, its mesmerizing birth of endless tautologies. Thus for Ernest the image captures the perpetual remapping of a structure in parts with jagged edges.

A Mandelbrot set seems to me not only an apt metaphor for fractals of African American literary histories as they began to emerge during the nineteenth century; it seems an apt description, too, of the challenges the black woman literary historian must confront if she would reconstruct the social landscape of a black and Native biographical subject, from the limited available resources of a memoir by a well-intentioned albeit supercilious white neophyte writer, and tax and court records either incomplete or preserved in now-outmoded legal discourse. Committed and conscientious Frances Whipple indubitably was as Elleanor Eldridge's coauthor; she was also patronizing in ways that betray a resolute conviction that whites were innately more intelligent than people of color. Furthermore, among the challenges of recovering and restoring *Memoirs of Elleanor Eldridge* is this greater complication: that African American literary history consists of both the complications introduced by the Whipples, Larisons, Stowes, and hundreds of other white interlocutors of black narrative performances as well as what Ernest (meditating on Barbara Christian's groundbreaking 1989 essay "The Race for Theory") has described as "an interactive process (sometimes characterized more by tension and conflict than by the collaboration of a coherent [black] collective) . . . the overlapping processes and practices that constitute nineteenth-century African American literary history" (*Chaotic Justice*, 21). The fears of whites clinging to institutional powers strive still to ensnare, using the old familiar images, desperate to control and contain the fates of women writers of color then and now—as narrators, authors, collaborators, and scholars, researchers, and consumers of life narratives—bound and born free. If ever they loosen their grip on the reins of power, one expects, the recovery of lives and narratives of the people of color from the early US republic would perhaps become a little easier. Luckily, Eldridge was able to take sufficient measure of Whipple's character and to work around the latter's elitism. From the collaboration of Eldridge's wit and grit, and Whipple's white power, a gift survives: *Memoirs of Elleanor Eldridge*.

Notes

1   "Marching Up the Heavenly Road," in *Black Song: The Forge and the Flame, the Story of How the Afro-American Spiritual Was Hammered Out*, ed. John Lovell, Jr. (New York: Macmillan, 1972).

2   Mary Ann Shadd Cary, "The Humbug of Reform," *The Provincial Freeman*, May 27, 1854. I am grateful to Elizabeth Cali for calling my attention to Shadd's polemic.

3   Hollis Read, *The Negro Problem Solved, or, Africa as She Was, as She Is, and as She Shall Be; Her Curse and Her Cure* (New York: A. A. Constantine, 1864).

4   Collins discusses white-developed controlling images of black women throughout chapter four of *Black Feminist Thought: Knowledge, Consciousness, and the Politics of Empowerment* (Boston: Unwin Hyman, 1990), 76–106.

5   Jane Lancaster, "A Web of Iniquity? Race, Gender, Foreclosure, and Respectability in Antebellum Rhode Island," *Rhode Island History* 69, no. 2 (2011): 82, 87n43.

6   Evelyn Brooks Higginbotham, "African-American Women's History and the Metalanguage of Race," *Signs* 17, no. 2 (Winter 1992): 251–74.

7   My thanks to my colleague Howard Rambsy II, who once pointed me to that passage in which Amiri Baraka and Larry Neal expressed the commercial white institutional publishing in *Black Fire*, ending their editors' note with the observation that "The frustration of working through these bullshit white people should be obvious" (*page #*). *Black Fire: An Anthology of Afro-American Writing*, 2nd ed., ed. Amiri Baraka and Larry Neal (New York: Morrow, 1969). See also the first editorial in *Freedom's Journal* (March 26, 1827, at New York City), which famously declared less than a decade before the publication of the first edition of *Memoirs of Elleanor Eldridge*, "We wish to plead our own cause." This is not to say that African Americans have not marginalized intraracially, using forms of restriction and discrimination, elitism and exclusivity ostensibly promoting "character" and respectability in the pursuit of "advancement," including sometimes, ironically, the stories of blacks whose achievements were gained with white assistance. See Xiomara Santamarina, "Thinkable Alternatives in African American Studies," *American Quarterly* 58, no. 1 (2006): 245–53.

8   Lois Brown, "Memorial Narratives of African Women in Antebellum New England," *Legacy* 20, no. 1 (2003): 38–61. The quoted passage is from 43.

9   Eldridge and Whipple, *Memoirs of Elleanor Eldridge* (1838), 27.

10   Birth and death dates for Dubois are as cited in *Speaking Lives, Authoring Texts: Three African American Women's Oral Slave Narratives*, ed. DoVeanna S. Fulton Minor and Reginald Pitts (Albany: State University of New York Press, 2009), 131.

11   Cornelius Wilson Larison uses the heading "Sylvia, A Free Negress" for one section of *Silvia Dubois, (Now 116 Years Old.) a Biografy of the Slav Who Whipt Her Mistres and Gand Her Fredom* (Ringos, NJ: C. W. Larison, 1883). The obituary

titled "A Free Negress" does not appear in the biography itself, of course, or in Fulton Minor and Pitts's edition of *Sylvia Dubois*. It is included as an unmarked, unnumbered appendix to the 1988 Oxford edition of *Sylvia Dubois*. Moreover, the obituary reprinted in the 1988 Oxford edition is, as Berthold notes, unsourced and undated (except for a handwritten "June 13, 1888" across the title heading line). Michael C. Berthold, "'The Peals of Her Terrific Language': The Control of Representation in 'Silvia Dubois, a Biografy of the Slav Who Whipt Her Mistres and Gand Her Fredom,'" *MELUS* 20, no. 2 (1995): 3–14. Fulton Minor and Pitts located what seems an earlier obituary for Dubois, dated June 2, 1888, in the Princeton, NJ, *Press*; it, in turn, cites the *Hopewell Herald* [Hopewell, NJ] as its source for confirming for readers that "Sylvia Dubois is at last really dead" (33n25, 26). Myths of African savagery differ according to gender, though there are some myths exclusively for black women and others solely circulated about men of African descent. The scholarship on these myths abounds; see, for example, Aliyyah I. Abdur-Rahman, *Against the Closet: Identity, Political Longing, and Black Figuration* (Durham: Duke University Press, 2012), and Janell Hobson, *Venus in the Dark: Blackness and Beauty in Popular Culture* (New York: Routledge, 2005).

12   For example, Dubois is not named in William L. Andrews, Frances Smith Foster, and Trudier Harris, eds., *The Oxford Companion to African American Literature* (New York: Oxford University Press, 1997); Joanne M. Braxton, *Black Women Writing Autobiography: A Tradition within a Tradition* (Philadelphia: Temple University Press, 1989); Paul Finkelman, ed., *Encyclopedia of African American History, 1619-1895: From the Colonial Period to the Age of Frederick Douglass*, 3 vols. (New York: Oxford University Press, 2006); *Africana: The Encyclopedia of the African and African American Experience*, ed. Kwame Anthony Appiah and Henry Louis Gates, Jr., 2nd ed., 5 vols. (New York: Oxford University Press, 2005); *A Shining Thread of Hope: The History of Black Women in America*, ed. Darlene Clark Hine and Kathleen Thompson (New York: Broadway Books, 1998).

13   See Brown's work, among others, on the power and importance of obituaries as a site of positive remembrance of women of African descent. On the archetypal bad black man and woman, see Trudier Harris, "History as Fact and Fiction," in *The Cambridge History of African American Literature*, ed. Maryemma Graham and Jerry Washington Ward (New York: Cambridge University Press, 2010), 451–96.

14   John Ernest, *Chaotic Justice: Rethinking African American Literary History* (Chapel Hill: University of North Carolina Press, 2009), 25.

15   Jean Fagan Yellin, ed., *The Harriet Jacobs Family Papers*. 2 vols. (Chapel Hill: University of North Carolina Press, 2008), xxv.

16   See, for example, P. Gabrielle Foreman, chapter one in *Activist Sentiments: Reading Black Women in the Nineteenth Century* (Urbana: University of Illinois Press, 2009), 19–42.

MEMOIRS

OF

ELLEANOR ELDRIDGE.

O that estates, degrees, and offices,
Were not derived corruptly! and that clear honor
Were purchased by the merit of the wearer!
How many, then, should cover, that stand bare?
How many be commanded, that command?
How much low peasantry would then be gleaned
From the true seed of honor? and how much honor
Picked frum the chaff and ruin of the times,
To be new varnished?—*Merchant of Venice.*

PROVIDENCE:
B. T. ALBRO—PRINTER,
1838.

PREFACE.

THIS little book⁣* is to be published for the express purpose of giving a helping hand to suffering and persecuted merit. And while its direct object is to render some little assistance to one who has been the subject of peculiar adversity and wrong, it may subserve a very important purpose, in bringing forward, and setting before the colored population, an example of industry and untiring perseverance, every way worthy their regard and earnest attention.—The numerous friends and patrons of poor Elleanor, are confident that the feeling and humane, to whom it gives the purest pleasure to alleviate misfortune, will cheerfully subscribe for her book, when they shall have received intimation of her singular claims upon their benevolence, both from her merit and her undeserved trials.

Still further, it is believed that the colored people, generally, will be proud to assist in sustaining one, who is both an honor and an ornament to their race.

The writer of these Memoirs must here crave the indulgence of Elleanor's patrons. The work is prepared during a season of severe illness, which has completely unfitted her for any exertion; and, in such a hurried manner, as to leave *no time for revision:* so that many important collateral principles, which might have been diffused through the work, enhancing its value, through her weakness, and want of time, must be neglected.

---

* This edition reprints *Memoirs of Elleanor Eldridge* from the original 1838 edition without any emendation or correction.

CHAPTER I.

To give some idea of the high esteem in which the subject of the following narrative is held, and the strong interest her misfortunes have excited, a few, from the great number of recommendations in her possession, are selected: and it may be well to present them in the onset, that all may be satisfied of the entire worthiness of her character, and credibility of her statements. These certificates were all voluntarily given, by the several ladies whose names are subjoined.

————

Having employed Elleanor Eldridge to work for me, occasionally, during the last sixteen years, at white-washing, painting, papering, &c. I can recommend her, as an honest, industrious, and faithful woman, who has been peculiarly unfortunate in the loss of her property, which she obtained by thirty years of hard labor. She has been unremitting in her exertions, to save enough to support herself in declining age, and invested all her savings in real estate, which was cruelly taken from her, while performing her duty in another State, as will appear in the history of her life. Had she remained in her native State, this dire misfortune might have been averted.

Elleanor has been truly unfortunate. She has suffered agony of body and mind. She has had every thing stripped from her, when she least expected it; and she was thrown upon the world, pennyless, after having cleared, on an average, more than one hundred dollars per annum, besides her support, during the thirty years above-mentioned, which, if placed at interest, annually, would have made her comparatively rich. She denied herself all, save the bare necessaries of life, to accomplish the desired end; yet she has been always ready to lend a helping hand to any of her relations who were needy, or in distress. She has been thro' life, and still is valuable to her numerous employers. She is a kind friend to those allied to her by the ties of blood; to whom, I believe, she never turned a deaf ear, or denied them relief which might be in her power to give.

The object in publishing her life, is to help raise a sum of money which MUST BE PAID, or she never can clear her property from its present incumbrance. She may be found, daily at work from sun-rise until sun-set, for good wages; yet she cannot accomplish the desired end, without the assistence of friends to humanity and justice. I hope a liberal public will patronise this work, for her sake, as well as that of her unfortunate race, who ought to be assisted rather than crushed, when they live a virtuous, industrious, and sober life, and not allowed to suffer wrongs, through their ignorance, that may be averted, by the timely assistance of the enlightened part of mankind.

A. G. D.

Providence, July 19, 1838.

—

WE, the undersigned, having known and employed Elleanor Eldridge to work for us during many years, recommend her as an uncommonly industrious woman—honest and faithful. We think her deserving to hold the property so dearly bought, with the hard labor of thirty years; and worthy a PREMIUM for her untiring perseverance to make herself independent of charity, when sickness, or old age should disable her to pursue her accustomed avocations.

> Anna Arnold,
> Anna Lockwood,
> Amey A. Arnold,
> Mrs. Elizabeth Elliot,
> Mrs. W. Rhodes,
> A. T. Lockwood,
> D. B. Lockwood,
> Mrs. E. G. Chandler,
> Mary T. Gladding,
> Mrs. H. Chandler,
> Mrs. H. Cushing.

This may certify that I have been acquainted with Elleanor Eldridge thirty-five years.—Twelve years she lived with Captain Benjamin Greene, at Warwick Neck, and made his dairy. She was at our house a number of times, to visit our colored woman. I think her to be a very respectable woman. This may also certify that I agree to the forgoing statement of Anna Lockwood and others.

Mrs. Nancy Webb.

Providence, July 20, 1838.

This is to certify that I have known Elleanor Eldridge for a number of years, and, during that time, I can truly say, that she has been a very industrious, prudent, and respectable woman; laboring early and late, to obtain, not only a livlihood, but a competency, that in her declining age she may not be dependant, upon the sympathies of a *cold, uncharitable* world, nor a pauper on her native town; which course, I think, is highly praisworthy. And as she has been wrongfully used, in regard to her property, I think it calls loudly to those friends who have employed her, for many years, and whose labors have given satisfaction, to endeavor at this present crisis, to lend a helping hand to the wants of suffering humanity; which can be done by subscribing for the little work, which is to be published, giving the history of her life; or by recommending her to the notice of the public, as one who ought to be encouraged, and patronised. She has worked for me during the last year at white-washing and papering, which have been done in the neatest manner; and I can recommend her as one who can be trusted to do the most delicate work in those branches; not only from my own experience, but reputation; I therefore would solicit, with others, the sympathies of the benevolent, in encouraging one who has literally obtained what little she possesses in the world, by the *sweat* of her *brow.* And if we by a little sacrifice, can render any service to one of our fellow beings, in the hour of affliction, we shall be abundantly recompensed, by the rich luxury of doing good; and answer in some degree, the design for which our Creator made us, *to do good*, as we have opportunity. I cordially give the above recommendation, and hope that the plans devised by her friends to secure her property, may meet with abundant encouragement and success.

Respectfully, yours,

July 28, 1838. MARY B. ANNABLE.

CHAPTER II.

It should not be considered essential to the interest and value of biography, that its subject be of exalted rank, or illustrious name. There is often a kind of ignus-fatuus light, playing around such names, calculated to dazzle and mislead, by their false lustre; until the eye can no longer receive the pure light of Truth, or the mind appreciate real excellence, or intrinsic worth. On the other hand, it often happens that, by lending our attention to the lowly fortunes of the indigent and obscure, important principles may be established, valuable truths elicited; and pure, and even lofty examples of virtue may be found. Then let no one turn with too much nicety from the simple story of the humble Elleanor, though it may contain few, or none, of the thrilling charms of poetry and passion.

Elleanor Eldridge, on the one hand, is the inheritress of African blood with all its heirship of wo and shame; and the subject of wrong and banishment, by her Indian maternity on the other. Fully, and sadly, have these titles been redeemed. It seems, indeed, as if the wrongs and persecutions of both races had fallen upon Elleanor.

She was born at Warwick, R. I., March 26, 1785. Her paternal grandfather was a native African. He was induced, with his family, to come on board an American slaver, under pretence of trade. With a large quantity of tobacco, prepared for barter, the simple-hearted African stepped fearlessly on board the stranger's ship, followed by his wife and little ones.

For some time he continued a friendly exchange of his staple commodity, for flannels and worsted bindings of gay and various colors. Already, in imagination, had his wife decorated herself with the purchased finery, and walked forth amid the villages, the envy and admiration of all the belles of Congo; and already had the honest African, himself, rivaled in splendor the princes of his land. Having finished his bargains, Dick, for that was the name of the Congo chieftain, proposed to return; but his hospitable entertainers would, on no account, allow him to depart without further attentions. Refreshments were handed freely about, with many little presents of small value. Then all the wonders of the ship, with the mysteries of operating its machinery, were to be explained to the intelligent, but uninformed stranger; while appropriate curiosities were displayed before the wondering eyes of his wife and children. By these means the confidence of the simple Africans was completely won.

Gaily the little ones danced along the buoyant deck, hardly restrained by their watchful and anxious mother; while ever and anon, they caroled sweet legends of their own sunny vales, blithe and careless as the sea-birds, which, even then, were skimming along the surface of the sea, ruffling the billowy tresses of the deep. Still the chief was detained; and still remained unsuspecting; until, to his utter horror, he found that his detainers, under pretence of illustrating some operation, had carefully weighed anchor, and were putting out to sea.

Vain were any attempt to depict the horrors of this scene. The African stood on the deck, with streaming eyes, stretching his arms out towards his own beautiful Congo; which lay, even then, distinctly visible, with the ruby light of sunset, stealing, like a presence of joy, through bower and vale, tinging the snowy cups of a thousand lilies. There too was his own beloved Zaire, stealing away from the distant forests of mangrove and bondo,* and flowing on within its lowly

* We cannot conclude this account of the principal vegetable productions of Lower Guinea, without mentioning that colossus of the earth, the enormous baobab, or Adansonia digitata, which is here called aliconda bondo and mapou. It abounds throughout the whole kingdom of Congo; and is so large that the arms of twenty men cannot embrace it.—*Maltebrun, on the authority of Tuchelli.* [This note and all subsequent footnotes were apparently written by Whipple, unless otherwise indicated.]

borders of tamarind and cedar, until, at last, it rushed into the arms of the Atlantic, troubling the placid bosom of the ocean with its tumultuous waters.*

Again he caught a gleam of his palm-roofed home, with all its clustering vines, from the rich forests of Madeira; its beautiful groves of cocoa and matoba, and its wide fields of masanga,† luno,‡ and maize; all waving richly beneath the bowing wind, rife with the promise of an abundant and joyful harvest. Beyond, in holy solitude, stood the tree of his worship, the sacred mironne,§ in its garments of eternal green, an apt emblem of the undying soul. He could almost see the tulip¶ groves where his children played; could almost see the light garlands of tube rose and hyacinth, their sportive hands had wreathed; with the rich clusters of nicosso** and tamba,†† they had gathered for their evening banquet. He could almost hear the murmurs of the home returning bees, as they lingered in the sweet groves of orange and pomegranate; for despair had quickened the senses: and a thousand objects, with all their thronging associations, came rushing to the mind, in that one agonizing moment, to quicken and aggravate its conceptions of eternal loss.

He stretched out his arms, and, in the agony of desperation, was about to leap into the sea, when his frantic wife, casting aside her screeching children, flung herself upon his bosom, and so restrained him. No sigh, no tear relieved him; but his bosom heaved convulsively; and the muscles and sinews became rigid, as if horror had

---

*The river Congo, called by the natives Zaire, or Zahire, is three leagues wide at its mouth; and empties itself into the sea with so much impetuosity, that no depth can there be taken.

† The masanga is a species of millet, highly pleasant both in taste and smell; the ears of which are a foot long, and weigh from two to three pounds.

‡ The luno forms a very white and pleasant bread, as good as that made of wheat. It is the common food of Congo.

§ The mironne of the same genus, (of the enzanda) is an object of adoration to the negroes.

¶ In every direction there are entire groves of tulips, of the most lively colors, intermixed with the tube-rose and hyacinth.

** The nicosso grows in clusters of the form of a pineapple.

†† The tamba is a species of bread fruit.—*Maltebrun.*

absolutely taken away the power of thought, or motion. The wife was more violent. With the most fearful cries she flung herself at the captain's feet and embracing his knees, begged for mercy. Then successively she embraced her weeping children; and at last, sank exhausted into the arms of her husband. It was all in vain. They were chained, and ordered below; where the sight of hundreds of wretches, stolen, wronged, wretched as themselves, only showed them that they were lost forever.

No tongue can depict the horrors of that passage. No imagination can form even a faint outline of its sufferings. Physical torture wrought its work. Humanity was crushed within them; and they were presented for sale, more than half brutalized for the brutal market. Few minds ever rise from this state, to any thing of their former rigor. The ancestor of Elleanor had one of these few; and though his pride was crushed, and his hopes forever extinguished, still he felt, and acted as a man.

But little more than the foregoing particulars is known to the subject of this narrative, concerning her ancestor, save that his African name was Dick; and that he had four children; one daughter Phillis; and three sons; Dick, George, and Robin; of whom the latter was her father.

At the commencement of the American Revolution, Robin Eldridge, with his two brothers, presented themselves as candidates for liberty. They were promised their freedom, with the additional premium of 200 acres of land in the Mohawk country, apiece.

These slaves fought as bravely, and served as faithfully, under the banner of Freedom, as if they had always breathed her atmosphere, and dwelt forever in her temple; as if the collar had never bowed down their free heads, nor the chain oppressed their strong limbs. What were toils, privations, distresses, dangers? Did they not already see the morning star of freedom, glimmering in the east? Were they not soon to exhibit one of the most glorious changes in nature? Were they not soon to start up from the rank of goods and chattels, into MEN? Would they not soon burst from the grovelling crysalis; and, spreading out the wings of the soul, go abroad in the glad sun-shine, inhaling the pure air of liberty?

Oh, LIBERTY! What power dwells in the softest whisper of thy syllables, acting like magic upon the human soul! He who first woke thy slumbering echoes, was a magician more potent than ever dwelt in the halls of genii; for he had learned a spell that should rouse a principle of the soul, to whose voice, throughout the wide earth, every human spirit should respond; until its power should be coextensive with the habitations of mind, and coeternal with its existence.

These poor slaves toiled on in their arduous duties: and while they literally left foot-prints of blood, upon the rough flint, and the crusted snow, they carried a fire within their bosoms which no sufferings could extinguish, no cold subdue—the God-enkindled fire of liberty.—They counted their perils and their sufferings joy, for the blessed reward that lay beyond.—Most dearly did they purchase and well they won the gift.

At the close of the war they were pronounced FREE; but their services were paid in the old Continental money, the depreciation, and final ruin of which, left them no wealth but the one priceless gem, LIBERTY.—They were free.—Having no funds, they could not go to take posession of their lands on the Mohawk. And, to this day, their children have never been able to recover them; though, by an act of Congress, it was provided, that all soldiers' children who were left incapable of providing for themselves, should "inherit the promises" due to their fathers. The subject of this memoir, attracted by an advertisement to this effect, attempted to recover something for a young brother and sister; but with the success which too often attends upon honest poverty, struggling with adverse circumstances. Her efforts were of no avail.

The spirit of Robin Eldridge was not to be broken down. Before entering the army he had married Hannah Prophet; and he now settled in Warwick, near the Fulling-Mill; where, by his honest industry, and general good character, he was always held in esteem. He soon became able to purchase land and build a small house; when he reared a large family, all of whom inherit their father's claims to the kindness and respect of those about them. He had, by this marriage, nine children; of whom Elleanor was the last of seven successive daughters. Of these children only five lived to mature age.

It may now be proper to look back a little, in order to glance at Elleanor's maternal ancestry. Her maternal grandmother, Mary Fuller, was a native Indian, belonging to the small tribe, or clan, called the Fuller family; which was probably a portion of the Narragansett tribe. Certain it is that this tribe, or family, once held great possessions in large tracts of land; with a portion of which Mary Fuller purchased her husband Thomas Prophet; who until his marriage, had been a slave. Mary Fuller, having witnessed the departing glories of her tribe, died in extreme old age, at the house of her son, Caleb Prophet; being 102 years old. She was buried at the Thomas Greene burying place in Warwick, in the year 1780. Her daughter Hannah, as we have said before, had been married to Robin Eldridge, the father of Elleanor.

Our heroine had the misfortune to lose her mother at the age of ten years; when she launched out boldly into the eventful life which lay before her, commencing, at once, her own self government, and that course of rigorous and spirited action, for which she has since been so much distinguished.

During her mother's life, it had often been her practice to follow washing, at the house of Mr. Joseph Baker, of Warwick; a daughter of whom, Miss Elleanor Baker, gave her own name to the little one she often carried with her; and always continued to take great interest in her little colored name-sake. Not long after the death of her mother, this young lady called on Elleanor, and invited her to come and reside with her, at her father's, offering her a home. She asked permission of her father, who consented, but with this remark, that she would not stay a week. The young heroine was not, however, to be so discouraged; but bravely collected herself, and began by making a definite BARGAIN with Miss Baker, before she consented to put herself under her protection, evincing, by this single act, a degree of prudence and wisdom entirely beyond her years. She fixed her price at 25 cents per week, and agreed to work for one year.

It was Sunday evening, in the changeful month of April, when Elleanor, with her whole wardrobe contained in the little bundle she held, stood with the family group she was about to quit forever. Let not the proud aristocrat smile disdainfully, because the biographer of poor Elleanor lingers a moment here. Home is home, to the lowly as well as the great; and no rank, or color, destroys its sacred character, its power over the mind, and the affections.—The sundering of family ties is always painful; and I have often thought that among the poor it is eminently so. There is nothing which strengthens the bonds of love so much as MUTUAL SUFFERING.

> "When joy has bound our hearts for years,
> A sudden storm those hearts may sever;
> But, Oh, the love that springs IN TEARS.
> Through time and change, endures forever;"

truly and beautifully says the poet. The ties, then, which unite families among the virtuous poor, are wrought from the deepest and strongest, and holiest principles of our nature. They have toiled, and struggled, and suffered together; until bond strengthens bond, and heart is knit with heart, by the strongest and most endearing ties. The world beyond and above, may persecute, oppress, and wrong them; yet out of these very circumstances springs a sympathy stronger than the great and the fashionable ever know. In the little sanctuary of a common house, all may gather themselves together and cherish this boon as their best treasure. Exterior to home the poor have no hope, no pleasure, no ambition, no desires; all the bliss of life is concentrated within its charmed circle; and, of necessity, its power is strong.

Our young heroine, having walked several times through the standing group, went again to the little nook in the chimney, where neatly ranged on their little shelves, were her playthings; shells and pebbles from the beach, little baskets made by her own hand; rag babies and acorns gathered from the wood. She loved these things more dearly than the children of the rich love their gilded toys; for they were full of the pleasant associations of her early childhood. She looked at them a moment, then turned and looked out of the window.—There was the little wood where she, with her happy brothers and sisters, had always played together, and in the bank close by the window, was her houses and ovens, with their sand pies and mud puddings, baking in clam and quahaug shells. She turned from the window, stooped to kiss the baby, that, with waddling steps, was trying to reach her favorite play-fellow, appearing to have an instinctive perception of something sad in the uncommon silence. The first to speak, for some minutes was the little brother then only five years old.

He sprung to his sister's arms, and clinging around her neck, cried "Dont go, Nelly! I play alone. I be tired. I cry!" and, suiting the action to the word, the poor little fellow burst into tears.

Elleanor swallowed, as well as she was able, the big lump that was rising in her throat, and comforted him with the promise of coming back soon.

"How long will be soon?" cried the child, still clinging to his sister, who was trying to disengage herself from him. "Will it be all night? Say Nelly?"

She could not answer; but placing her hands silently in those of her two elder sisters, and pausing a moment before her father, she turned from the door, wiped the tears away with the corner of her short-gown, and ran along the road quite fast, to escape the earnest cries of her weeping brother.

The heart of childhood is always buoyant; and that of Elleanor was soon bounding lightly again; for ambitious projects were, even then, beginning to germinate in her young bosom.—She paused at a turn in the road, which gave her a last view of the cottage; and, looking back a moment she wiped another tear away; and resumed her walk. The distance was two miles; and Elleanor reached there before sunset. She was kindly received, even by the old dog and house cat; but she felt somewhat disinclined for society, and she soon begged permission to retire to her little bed; where her slumbers were soft and sweet, as if she had slept on a bed of down, garnished with the most splendid drapery. Blessed are the slumbers of the innocent! They are kindlier than balm; and they refresh and gladden the spirit of childhood, like ministerings from a better world.

CHAPTER III.

The new relation into which Elleanor had entered, tended to produce mutual satisfaction to the parties sustaining it. Kindness and good feeling, on the part of employers, seldom fail to seeure industry and fidelity, in that of the employed. When a mistress, and the several members of her family, manifest an interest in the welfare of their servants—when they show them that they are considered as human beings, belonging to the same great family of man—that the common rights of humanity are understood and regarded—that those who perform their servile labors are members of the same family, sustaining certain relations, and filling certain places (by no means unimportant ones) in the gradations of society—and are *not the mere instrnments of their own selfish gratification*—created to administer to their pleasures; the interests of the serving and the served, generally become identified; and the heart quickens and strengthens the hands in the performance of duty. Those who are governed by these principles know their weight and force; sorrowful it is to think, that the world will not also learn that kind and judicious masters and mistresses, generally are blessed with efficient and faithful servants. I, by no means, intend to lay all the follies, vices, and crimes of servants at the door of their employers; but I am persuaded that the comforts, rights, and, more especially, the *moral health* of domestics is shamefully neglected. Instead of being treated as accountable beings—as persons indeed, capable of independent thought, feeling, and action—susceptible alike of pleasure and pain, they are considered as the mere appendages of luxury; and being generally left to their own wayward courses, often sink into depravity and vice, when a little of kindness and good feeling, a little affectionate interest and judicious advice, might restrain and save them.—Let them who think lightly of these things, consider the immense value of a single human being! Were this considered, and acted upon, a reformation in the department of domestic service, would soon begin; and the blessings which would flow from it, would be greater than a superficial thinker might be made to believe *could* proceed from such a source. But enough of this.

With the early dawn Elleanor was seen, dashing away the dews with her little bare feet, as she drove the cows to pasture; all the time singing blithely, as the birds themselves. She always had a provident eye on the poultry and the happiest art of finding their hiding-places. No hen's nest throughout all the varieties of place, stable, hay-loft, wood-pile, thicket, meadow, or out-building, escaped her searching eye. She won the confidence of her feathered friends so entirely, by her zealous attention to their wants that she could, with all the *sang froid* of her Indian character, cross the path of some sly old turkey, about starting to her nest, without exciting the least apprehension; and, with apparent listlessness and unconcern, watching all the artful doublings and windings of that wary foul, she would soon start, with a light step, to her chosen sanctum, and so make herself mistress of the poor turkey's secret *sans ceremonie*. In such cases when she returned with her course apron laden with the mottled treasure, she always men such a warm smile, as was, at once, a reward for the present, and incentive to the future. Not only the family, but every living creature about the house and farm, loved little Elleanor. The dog and cat, the horses, cows, pigs, sheep and poultry, all knew her light step, and in their several ways manifested their love. And well they might; for when they were well, she fed them; and when they were sick, she nursed them; and she always took the kindest care of the young and helpless.

At the expiration of the year, Elleanor received her wages, and commenced a new term of service for 2s. per week.

The marriage, and consequent removal, of her young mistress, to whom she was tenderly attached, was a great trial to her; and for some time she was very melancholy and home-sick; but she recovered, at length, her usual degree of cheerfulness.

With this kind family she remained five years and nine months. During that time she learned all the varieties of house-work and every kind of spinning; and in the last year she learned plain, double, and ornamental weaving, in which she was considered particularly expert. This shews that our heroine has great mechacical genius; or, to speak phrenologically, that her "constructiveness," "comparison," and "calculation" are well developed. This double weaving, as it is called—i.e. carpets, old fashioned coverlets, damask, and bed-ticking, is said to be a very difficult and complicated process; and I presume there are few girls of fourteen, capable of mastering such an intricate business; and when we consider that she was entirely uneducated; that her powers had never been disciplined by any course of study, it seems really wonderful that she could enter into this difficult business, at that early age, with so much spirit and success. Yet she was, at the expiration of the year, pronounced a competent and fully-accomplished weaver.

In the commencement of her sixteenth year, Elleanor took leave of her kind patrons, and went to live next at Capt. Benjamin Greene's, at Warwick Neck, to do their spinning for one year.

At the expiration of the year she was engaged as dairy woman. It appears really wonderful that any person should think of employing a girl, but just entering her seventeenth year, in this nice and delicate business. Yet so it was; and the event proves that their judgment was correct. Elleanor continued in this situation eight years. She took charge of the milk of from twenty-five to thirty cows; and made from four to five thousand weight of cheese annually. Every year our heroine's cheese was distinguished by A PREMIUM.

We acknowledge to the sentimentalist that these matters are not very poetical; but to the lover of truth, they are important, as giving a distinct idea of the capacity, which early distinguished our subject.

About the period of her nineteenth year, Elleanor became quite a belle; and her light foot in the dance, and her sweet voice in the song, made her an object of great interest among the colored swains. Sad indeed was the havoc which the sweet singing, and the more exciting movements of the dance, wrought among their too susceptible hearts!

Whether Elleanor, herself, ever yielded to the witching influence of the tender passion, remains in the Book of Mysteries to this day.

Sometimes, with a low, quick breath—I could almost imagine it a sigh—she would say, "There was a young man—I *had* a cousin—He sent a great many letters—" but further our deponent saith not. Not a syllable more could I ever extract from her. I have asked her for the letters; which, being her veritable biographer, I had a right to do; but she always tells me they are in a great box, with all the accumulated weight of her household stuff resting upon them. Now, dearest reader, if I can ever extract aught further touching this delicate and pleasing subject, I will not fail to make you acquainted with it; or if I can, by any persuasion, get a peep at any letters from the cousin afore-mentioned, I hereby pledge myself that you too shall be advised of their contents.

And now, as darkness is closing fast around me, I beg leave to retire from your pleasant company; and so I wish you a very good evening.

CHAPTER IV.

As was remarked in the preceding chapter, Elleanor, at this period, was a belle. During her residence at Capt. Greene's, it seems that her brother, Mr. George Eldridge, had been chosen Governor of the colored election; and was re-elected three successive years. As this title was, in imitation of the whites, invested with considerable dignity, it follows that Elleanor stood among her people, in the very highest niche of the aristocracy. She always accompanied her brother to these festivals, dressed in such style as became the sister of "His Excellency." On some of these occasions she wore a lilac silk; on others a nice worked cambric; then again a rich silk, of a delicate sky blue color; and always with a proper garniture of ribbons, ornaments, laces, &c.—I trust I have acquitted myself, with all honorable exactness, in regard to the dresses; seeing it is important to the world that it should be enlightened on this subject; and no fair reader of marvellous tales, I am confident, would ever forgive me, should I neglect to say in what guise our heroine appeared abroad; for such a course would be entirely without precedent; and I feel no disposition to introduce a new system. Although I speak of Elleanor in this light, let no one think her story is fictitious; she is none the less a *heroine* because it is *true*.

At the period to which we now refer, Elleanor was light-hearted, and free from shadow as the fairest morning; with the sweet sensations of a happy and benevolent nature quickening within her bosom, like spirits of joy, that tinged all she looked upon with the hues of their own lights and gladness,

"But all that's bright must fade,
The fairest still the fleetest;
All that's sweet, is made
  But to be lost when sweetest."

And so passed away the "dancing days" of Elleanor; bright as the
morning rainbow, and like that, too, the presage of darkness and storms.

No doubt, my fair readers are in a state of highly wrought expec-
tancy in regard to the *affair du cœur*, of which I barely hinted in the
last chapter. Happy am I, to communicate the pleasing intelligence, of
new arrivals from that quarter. To descend, at once, from the language
of metaphor, to that of plain, sober fact, I rejoice to say that a portion
of the correspondence, above alluded to, together with certain facts
explanatory thereof, has been laid before me; and, in all confidence, as
if the reader were my bosom friend, I hasten to fulfil the promise tendered in the last chapter.

I must beg leave to premise, dear reader, that you shall endeavor to
be satisfied with the knowledge of these facts, making no single question concerning them; as I shall, in no wise, feel myself bound to explain
any thing in regard to the circumstances by which I became possessed
of them.

The manuscripts came to me in much the same order and connection, as that in which the Editor of Sartor Resartus, found those of
the lamented sage and philosopher, Teufelsdroch, when he found out
the contents of the Bag Capricornus; when milk bills, love ditties, laun-
dress' bills, poetry, with torn and yellow scrips of paper, containing all
high and unimaginable thoughts and reflections, came tumbling in a
heap together. There may be, in deed, no further comparison between
them: and it may be hinted, even, that Elleanor's documents want the
pith and marrow contained in those of Teufelsdroch; but of this I am
no bound to speak, since my province is not criticism, but narration.

Let us turn aside, then, for a short time, from the straight-forward
path of history, into the pleasant regions of episode; where, as in a little
grotto apart from the high road, we may indulge in an hour of repose;
turning, meanwhile, to the simple story for amusement. Having thus so
comfortably established ourselves, wich no evil-minded eaves-dropper

to make us afraid; bend now, dear reader, thy most earnest and delicately adjusted ear; for I am going to tell thee A SECRET.

Let us come directly to the subject matter in point. Elleanor, when a buxom lassie of eighteen, by some means or other, became acquainted with a lad somewhat older than herself, whom we shall designate as Christopher G——, though whether this was the whole, or any part of his real name, or one chosen as a screen, behind which to conceal the blushes of the sensitive Elleanor, is a subject upon which I have no liberty to speak. So this also may be passed over to the budget of MYSTERIES.—Let us, dear reader, remember the punishment of idle curiosity, as taught in the true and affecting history, yeclept "Blue Beard;" and, striving to be content with the facts in the case, seek not to lift the veil, which the sensibility of true love, and feminine delicacy, have alike conspired to draw.

This Christopher, I have found by a course of induction, the process of which has nothing to do with this story, to be the same true and veritable person, of whom Elleanor speaks so plaintively, and so pithily, when she said: "I HAD A COUSIN." How much is told in those four little words. They are, of themselves, a history. They contain all the regular parts of a true epic; viz: beginning, middle, and end; together with outlines, circumstances, and decorations. We need only shut our eyes; and lo, as if the lamp of Aladelin were lighted in our presence, all the mysteries stand unveiled before us, in their true order and connection. But as every one of my readers may not be gifted, in the highest degree, with the organs of ideality and "language," I make no doubt they will prefer a translation to the original, especially as I am enabled to enrich that translation, with numerous notes, coming from a not-to-be-doubted source.

Certain it is that the youthful cousins, even in the very first interview, began to suspect, (or might have began to suspect, were not love blind, so that frequently he does not know his own image,) that there are dearer ties than those of consanguinity.

There was the due proportion of fear, hope, doubt, ecstacy, and moonlight; together with the proper infusion of sighs, tears, &c., "for all such cases made and provided," until, at length, the important and accustomed tender, was made, listened to—and—accepted. Thus far, all was well. There was the light of hope in the eye of Elleanor, and her footstep had the grace and buoyancy of joy.

Often did the lovers meet, (I feel myself justified in calling them so, since I find all the features of a most undoubted case,) and in the stillness of those beautiful solitudes, which surrounded them, they breathed their vows; unlooked upon, save by the kind moon, and the gentle stars, which, I believe all will agree, are far the best witnesses on such occasions. In the silent grove, and by the solemn sea, they wandered for hours together, creating to themselves a world of fairy-like beauty, which the confidence of loving hearts, warmed and kindled into truth.

> "All lovely things grew lovelier. The flowers
> Bloomed with more vivid brightness, and the grass
> Caught a more pleasant greenness, than of yore.
> The winds that bowed the forest, or breathed low,
> With a sweet voice of sadness to the flowers,
> Still spoke to their affections; while the moon
> Grew kindlier, and came nearer to the heart,
> Like the familiar presence of a friend.
> The waters and the birds sang, aye, of love;
> Or seemed to chant the story of *their* loves;
> While all the stars had feeling in their light,
> Like the expressive eyes of sympathy.
> Even in the holy silence of the wood,
> When not a wind was breathing, a low voice
> Came with a blessing to their conscious hearts;
> For the sweet presence of undoubting Love,
> Spake to the soul, and these was audible."

And were they poor? No. They had found that which the wealth of kings could not purchase—"the pearl of great price"—the gem of LOVE—and it was safely treasured in the casket of faithful and all-believing hearts.

Then came the first parting, with the mutually reiterated vows of everlasting truth and remembrance; and the succeeding night of wakefulness and tears. But the shadow of absence had scarcely glanced over the fair heaven of Elleanor, when a sunbeam of a letter came: and all was bright again. The letter was as follows

From Christopher G. to his Cousin.
NEWPORT, March 27, 1805.

My dearest Cousin:

I have thought of you, almost with one thought, since I left. How strange it is that wherever I look I see nothing but my dear Ellen. I am well; but my heart is heavy; for I miss the dear eye that always looked on me in kindness; and I don't like to think there may be many weeks before I see you again.—When in Warwick I thought one week was a great while; but now I must learn to bear the pain of absence. I have lately been to the white Election; and I was astonished and disgusted with the behaviour I saw among the whites. I think the white people ought to be very careful what they do, and try to set good examples for us to follow; for whatever they do, whether good or bad, the colored people are sure to imitate them. I am glad that you, my dear cousin, do not, like some of your companions, attempt to follow all the extravagant fashions of the white people. If we are ever to rise above our present condition, fine clothes will not enable us to do it.

My mind remains the same that it was the last time I talked with you; so this is hoping you are well and happy.

From your affectionate cousin, and true lover.

CHRISTOPHER G———.

This letter was "little; but 'twas all she wished;" and it passed directly from the heart to the memory; and there it is treasured, even to this day.

Next came the blissful first reunion of loving hearts, with the halcyon wing of Hope shedding the brightness of its plumage over them.

There are many things fondly cherished in the history of love; but the first parting, and the first reunion, are embalmed with the holiest tears of memory and hope: and their greenness is kept forever.

But we must not dwell too long amid these tender scenes, which, indeed, exert a kind of witchery over the heart, making it fain to linger.

CHAPTER V.

Now must we return again to the high way; and so most courteous reader, if you are rested from the toils which I have hitherto called you to endure, let us leave this pleasant subject for a while, for one of minor interest, if not of like importance.

At the age of nineteen, Elleanor was again called to mourn over the departure of another kind parent. She lost her father; and a sad loss it was to her; for Robin Eldridge had the art, which many white fathers have not, that of commanding, at once, respect and affection.

As the deceased had left property, letters of administration were taken out; but it was soon found that the estate could not be settled, without some legal advices from a daughter, then residing in the north-western part of Massachusetts. In this crisis, what was to be done? The delays and difficulties attending a communication by mail, were of themselves sufficiently objectionable; and to hire a person to go there, would be a greater expense than the little estate would justify. At this point Elleanor came forward and offered her services, which were gladly accepted.

With a spirit worthy one of the nation of Miantonomies, she set off, on foot and alone, to make a journey of 180 miles. It may be asked where, at this period was the gallant Christopher?

Months had passed on, with variety of interest or feeling, until at length Christopher, like his immortal name-sake, went forth to try his fortune on the great deep. The farewell, "a word which hath been and must be," was breathed, and listened to, with a feeling of sorrow they had not hitherto dreamed of: and the parting scene was over. Perhaps it was the peculiar state of mind and feeling, induced by this event, which tempted Elleanor to try the excitement of new scenes. It is certain that all her familiar haunts wore an aspect of strange loneliness; and the gladliest things, even those which were wont to give her the greatest pleasure, grew sad and melancholy.

Elleanor had obtained leave of her kind mistress to be absent for a short time, and she returned home to make arrangements for her departure. The evening before she set off on her journey, Elleanor had completed all her preparations; and, with her sister, was sitting over a good fire; for the chilly evenings of September had begun; talking over the probable adventures of her pilgrimage, and the event of the business which was its occasion; receiving also kind messages from the friends she left, for those whom she expected to see, when her brother entered. Was there something peculiar in his appearance? Was there anything marked or uncommon in his manner, that Elleanor trembled and turned pale? Or was it by the mysterious intuition of love, that she felt the approach of one of its revalutions; with a kind of electric sensibility, as steel is troubled at the coming tempest, before a cloud can be discerned by the physical eye? I will not venture to account for the reason. With the fact only have I to do. Certain it is that Elleanor suddenly broke off the sentence she was speaking; and was seized with an inexplicable fit of trembling; which in no wise abated, when her brother, as if with preconcerted moderation, put his hand in his pocket; and said, with an expression of unconcern, "Here—is—a—letter—from—"

"From Cristopher?" said his sister Fettina; pronouncing the name that hovered inaudibly on the lips of Elleanor.

"I believe so;" said he, producing a folded paper. "Here, Ellen, I suppose this belongs to you."

She took the letter; and here, even as if we were privileged to look over her shoulder, let us read it.

East Greenwich, August 27, 1805.
My dearest Ellen—I cannot go away without improving the present opportunity of saying a few words more to you. I have got a voyage from Providence, where I expect to go in a few days. I hope you will not

tremble for me, and be unhappy every time the wind blows; for I shall then be far away from all the danger that you can know any thing about. I am going to the West Indies; and if I do my duty, and have tolerable luck, I shall be in a way to make something. Let us not think of troubles; for thinking of them beforehand will never make them lighter when they come. If God permit, I shall return in the course of a few months; and then we shall meet again, and be happy.—It may be wrong, but it seems to me that I almost feel a pleasure in this parting from you, for had it not been, I should not have guessed how dear I am to you. I am in good health; and hope these few lines will find you enjoying the same blessing. So, praying we shall meet again, no more at present; and I remain your best beloved, till death.

CHRISTOPHER G——.

There are some adventitious circumstances which minister so directly to the necessities of the occasion, as almost brings a conviction that they are providential. So Ellen, at this very point of time, when she would soon have been beyond its reach; in fact, in almost the only hour whe shen could have done so, for some months, received her cousin's letter; and it seemed, really, as if a special Providence smiled upon her love: and with this pleasant tho't she fell into a sweet slumber; when the spirits of Elysium came and ministered around her.

Before day-break our heroine was stirring.—She dressed herself in a coarse and rather old gown, and bonnte, to correspond with her pedestrian style of travelling; while she carefully wrapped another, and better suit, in a bundle; which the fair and romantic reader will remember, a heroine never fails to take.

But Elleanor was more provident, and, withal, more reasonable, than the fair Cherubina, when disgusted with the happiness of her own paternal home, she went in search of misfortunes; for she took only a guinea, fearing very justly, that if she had plenty of money she could not so soon fall into those amiable and irresistibe distresses, she so often met with in the thrilling histories of romantic miseries, of every sort and fashion, which were her favorite reading; and which she never failed to weep over, with all suitable demonstrations of sorrow. Indeed she, like many others, put herself to such expense of sympathy for these beings of the imagination, that she had none to bestow on REAL SUFFERING. Pardon this digression, dear reader. It was involuntary. I had began to say that Elleanor, unlike the heroine above alluded to, took the good substantial sum of sixty dollars; which she carefully concealed about her person, in case of sickness or accident. But being afraid to appear to have money, she solicited the kind charities of those among whom she passed; and only now and then, paid a few cents for a night's lodging.

The last letter of Christopher, with the talismanic charm of true love, went with her; and often, when she paused to rest by the way-side, she drew it forth; and dwelt with a sort of awe upon its mystic characters; with which her heart-quickened memory had associated all their true meaning; and, at such periods, many a thought, if thought could be visible, might have been seen winging its way far to the south-east, unchecked by the barriers of ocean.

Such was the dignity and general propriety of her carriage and behaviour, that she went on unmolested; accomplishing her journey safely and honorably, as the Milesian nymph, of whom Moore has sweetly sung.

"On she went; and her maiden smile
In safety lighted her round the green Isle;
And blessed forever is she who relied
Upon Erin's honor, and Erin's pride."

In the course of her journey she came one night to an Inn, where she found them preparing "entertainment" for a large company.—They were short of "help;" and very gladly availed themselves of our heroine's services, who entered into their arrangements, at once, with her accustomed spirit and success; acquitting herself of her duties in a very superior style.—At this house she remained during the next day and night; and when she left, her kind hostess furnished her with such provisions as she could carry.

At the end of five days Elleanor reached the house of her aunt, her mother's only sister, who resided in Adams. She with her family, was so much surprised to see Elleanor, she could scarcely believe the evidence of her own senses. But when they found that it was even so, all were overjoyed. So they called in her sister, and all her cousins, and killed, not "the fatted calf;" but what is better, a good fat turkey and the happiness of that day was like the light of a summer sun, when there was no cloud on the the face of heaven.

And here, dear reader, it is fitting Elleanor should take a little rest, after her long and toilsome journey. So, with your permission, we will bid her adieu for the present.

CHAPTER VI.

Our heroine visited all her relations, of whom there were many, all respectable, and well established in the world; and finally, as the cold weather had already commenced, she concluded to stay until spring. She found some of her old neighbors from Warwick there, who received her among them very cordially. She could not long remain idle; and she soon found plenty of business. She engaged herself as a weaver in the family of Mr. Brown; and subsequently, in the same business, to that of Mr. Bennett; where she remained till spring. This period was enlivened by many balls and parties, at all of which Elleanor took a conspicuous part. She, indeed, made quite a sensation among the colored beaux of Adams; but for reasons which my reader knows, and they did not, their advances met with such a cool return they durst not renew the subject. Ah, dear reader! we may see by this, that Elleanor, though a belle, was no flirt. Great, indeed, was the wonder how she could be so entirely indifferent to attention, which the best among them were sighing for; and all enquired the reason; and none could give it: at least, none *did* give any thing like the true reason, until an arrival from Warwick, brought another letter from Christopher, which, coming as it did all the way from the West Indies, the good people there looked upon it with much the same feelings with which we survey what is called a "moon stone,"—as a direct communication from another sphere. I said they looked *upon* the letter, dear reader; but not a single one of them looked *into* it, as we shall do, except her cousin, and bosom confidant, Ruth Jacobs. Here we have the letter.

From Christopher to his cousin.
St. Pierre, Gaudaloupe, Nov. 20, 1805.

My own true love—Though I am now far—very far away from you, and the raging sea is now rolling between us; yet I think of you, if possible, more than I did when at home. I am in good health, which God grant may be the happy case with you, and all the dear friends I have left. I have met with various misfortunes since I saw you. Once I have been pressed into the English service, and once cast away. But I have had the good fortune to escape from both these troubles; and when we meet, I will then speak more fully of these matters, than I have time to do at present. I must hasten to finish this, to send by our old neighbor, Mr.——, who is just going to sail for Providence. He will visit Warwick: and has promised to give this to you with his own hand. I should have been able to send you some present, if I had not met with the misfortunes above-mentioned. I expect to go from this port in a few days, to the island of ——, where I intend to change my employment; and, as I hope, for the better. I advise you to keep up good spirits; for every thing that has passed from me to you in the way of words, I consider sacred: and, if it please God that I return, all shall be fulfilled. You may expect to hear from me again soon; and in the mean time I rest—

Your loving and true—
CHRISTOPHER G——.

This letter was the gossip's wonder for the month to come. Wonders live more than nine days, amid the abundant nutriment and healthy air of the country; and it was the secret joy and pride of Elleanor, long, long after.

In the spring, having procured legally executed letters from her sister, investing her with the power of attorney to receive all goods, chattels, and monies, in her name, our heroine took leave of her kind employers and entertainers, and left Adams. She had the good fortune to get passage with Mr. Bennett as far as Northampton, whither he was going to market.

Finally, she reached home in health and safety; and, having accomplished the object of her errand, the estate was soon satisfactorily settled.

Elleanor returned to her service at Capt. Greene's.

No tidings of Christopher, since the letter received at Adams, had been received for months; and it is not strange that sundry doubts, misgivings, and fears, of a very tender and interesting nature, occasionally weighed down the hitherto light heart of Ellen, with unwonted heaviness. However, no private feelings of her own, lessened her attention to her several duties. It seemed, indeed, as if she sought to engross herself more completely than ever, with the bustle of business; for Ellen, though she knew it not, was a practical philosopher—at least, experience taught her one truth—that THE BEST REMEDY FOR SORROW IS OCCUPATION.

Weeks had rolled on since her return, and June had come, with its leafy bowers and its woodland music. On a pleasant evening, in that sweetest of all seasons, Elleanor, having finished the business of the day, walked out on a green, ostensibly to look at some pieces of cloth which were spread there to bleach; but really to indulge the feelings, which were so equally ballanced by joy and sorrow, that she could not have told whether she were most sad, or happy. The peaceful hour of twilight came on, when the heart instinctively gathers up its memories, and withdrawing the curtain of the past, snatches, as it were some dying flowers from the cold altar of Oblivion. The spirit of the hour was tenderness. From tenanted bough and peopled hive, came the low sweet murmur of bird and insect; while the soft bleating of flocks, and the low of kine went up at intervals from fold and pasture. Even the grasshopper's note had lost its sharpness; and it went trilling along though his green fastnesses, as if a thousand spirits were touching the fibres of the grass, and drawing forth its hidden music.—Then there were momentary pauses of such deep and exquisite stillness, that the falling of the dew was almost audible, as it went forth on its ministry of love, to kiss the drooping flower and invigorate the thirsty leaf.

Elleanor stood before the goodly pieces of linen, which were spun and woven by her own hand, and might have done honor to her art; but the vivid contrast of the whitened fabric, upon the beautiful ground of green, had no effect upon her eye; for she saw it not. She was wandering far away on the wing of thought, over isle and billow; and from that peaceful scene her spirit had flown away, and hung hovering over the tempestuous sea. Her heart had begun to feel that sickness, that cometh from "hope deferred." For long months she had heard nothing of her cousin; and now, when there were none to know, or to mock her feelings, is it strange that yielding to the softness of the scene, she could not check the burst of tenderness that sprung unbidden in her heart. She sat down upon a stone, and leaning her head upon her hand, presently the pent up tears burst from their confines, and she wept. With low and scarcely articulated tones, she unconsciously breathed the name that was dearest; and so absorbed—so completely wrapt was she, that she heard not an advancing step, and felt not conscious of the presence of another, until a low sigh responded to her own; and certain well remembered tones modulated to the syllables of her own name arrested her attention—

"Ellen!"

She looked up. It was no illusion. As if the very magic of her thought had drawn him there, her cousin Christopher was standing before her. "Ellen!" he repeated.

"Christopher!" was the low and deep response.

And here, dear reader the curtain drops;—since it is not meet that the sacred scene should be witnessed by the cold eye of a stranger.

CHAPTER VII.

We come now suddenly to a gap of several years in the data of our manuscripts; though, without a doubt, there is none on the transcript kept by the memory of Ellen. There might be read, if the scroll could come before the eye, the record of many sad partings, and many glad returns; each, and all, giving an additional fibre, to the bonds of love, which like a vine, had clung from heart to heart, growing and strengthening while it united them.

We come now to the last letter which we are permitted to see.

From Christopher to his Cousin.
Archangel, June 30, 1811.

Dear Ellen—

I am very sorry I could not write to you before, on account of being pressed on board of a Man of War. I have suffered many things; yet my chief trouble was the fear that I might never return to my dear Ellen, and be permitted to realise all those sweet hopes, and earnest promises, I have so often indulged in. I have been to Dublin, and I expect to sail for England in the course of a month; and then I shall return home as quick as possible. My health is very good—thanks to God for it!—and may this find you, as well as it leaves me. You must not be uneasy about me, as I hope the time will not be long before I see you again.—Give my love to my cousins, and all enquiring friends. So no more at present, from your ever loving and affectionate

Christopher G——.

This Letter wrought its good work upon the half-desponding Elleanor. She went cheerfully again about her duties, while she kept all these pleasant sayings hid from those about her, secretly cherishing and pondering them in her heart.

Again was she happy in the blissful presence of him she loved; but her happiness was chastened by the anxieties which had stolen in, like shadows, upon the sun-light of her affections.

In remembering the solicitudes of the past, she drew a picture of the future; and involuntarily looked forward to another course of doubts and fears which ever beset those who have friends upon the deep.

After a series of pleasant visits, which enlivened the period of Christopher's stay, he attended her to the Newport Election, where the gaieties of the present scene, could not illumine the coming sorrow, which already had cast its shadow before her: and she really felt it a relief to return home, where they arrived late on Saturday evening.

Little sleep had poor Elleanor that night; for the morrow was to be the day of parting: and she rose unrefreshed from her pillow. At an early hour her gallant was in attendance; and the day passed away in pleasant, but rather constrained conversation, with the family, and some cousins, who had assembled themselves on the occasion.

But in the evening, at an early hour, Christopher and Elleanor found themselves beneath the very oak, which had been hitherto the scene of every parting. Twilight passed into evening. The moon rose, and the stars came forth; yet still he lingered. The sorrowful thought of separation was too strong—too deep for words; but each looked upon the face of the other with that earnest and solemn meaning, which tells of the heart's acutest anguish. Never had the thought of parting been so bitter. Again and again did he attempt to go; until, at length, with desperate energy, he wrung her hand; and fuming away quickly, as if he would not trust himself with another look, he was gone in a moment. Elleanor sat down with a heaviness of heart she had never before known; but tears came not to her relief.

But we must not dwell on this interesting episode. That "The course of true love never *did* run smooth"—has become a truism almost; and in the case of Elleanor, certainly it proved true.

There was a long period of alternating hopes, doubts, and distressing fears. Then came the heart-rending intelligence, of shipwreck, and death.

But the image of her first, and only love, was shrined within the faithful heart of Elleanor.—In her loneliness she cherished it; and in solitude poured out her tears upon its consecrated altar.

Elleanor remained at Capt. Greene's until 1812, being then twenty-seven years old. At this time the death of Capt. G. occasioned alterations in the family; so our heroine returned home to live with her oldest sister Lettise, who had been appointed by the Court of Probate, as guardian to the younger children; and filled a mother's place in the care of the whole family.

Elleanor now, with her sister, entered into a miscellaneous business, of weaving, spinning, going out as nurse, washer, &c.—in all of which departments she gave entire satisfaction; and in no single instance, I believe, has failed to make her employers friends. She also, with her sister, entered considerably into the soap boiling business. Of this article they every year made large quantities, which they brought to the Providence market, together with such other articles as they wished to dispose of, or as were, with suitable commissions, supplied by their neighbors. By this time the earnings of Elleanor had amounted to a sum sufficient to purchase a lot and build a small house, which she rented for forty dollars a year.

During the time of her residence with her sister, being at work at Mr. Gordon Arnold's, she received the afflicting intelligence of the sudden death of one of her brother's children, and the extremely dangerous illness of another.

When she arrived at his house, she found that two children were already dead,—and a third lay apparently at the point of death; and indeed only lived till the next morning. A fourth child was seized with the same symptoms; but, after lingering for three weeks, recovered.— Thus three children were taken from the midst of health; and all in the space of forty-eight hours. It was supposed that they had eaten some poisonous substance, which they had found in a swamp where they often went, and had mistaken for birch. It was indeed a most distressed family; and Elleanor found it difficult to sustain them under their severe losses.

She remained with her sister three years;—and was then induced by another sister, who resided here, to come to Providence; where she soon arrived and commenced a new course of business, viz—white-washing, papering, and painting; which she has followed for more than twenty years, to the entire satisfaction of her numerous employers.

The above occupations she generally followed nine or ten months in the year; but commonly, during the most severe cold of winter, she engaged herself for high wages, in some private family, hotel, or boarding house. Two of these winters she worked at Mr. Jackson's;—and the two following at Governor Taft's; and it is worthy of remark, and alike creditable to herself, and her employers that ELLEANOR HAS ALWAYS LIVED WITH GOOD PEOPLE.

The next winter after this she went to New York, and worked for Miss Jane C———. She liked very much; and the succeeding winter also found her in New York. But at this time she had the misfortune to catch a severe cold occasioned by the damps of the basement kitchen, which threw her into a malignant fever, of the typhus kind. The kind Miss C——— treated her with the most generous and affectionate attention; indeed, as if she had been one of her own family. She had an excellent nurse provided, and two of the most skilful physicians the city afforded; with every delicacy that gives comfort to the chamber of the sick.

After remaining for some time in a state of the most imminent danger, the strength of a vigorous constitution shook off the disease; and she began slowly to recover.

On the first of April she took leave of the benevolent Miss C———, and returned to Providence; when that lady, with a generosity almost unparalleled in this selfish world, after discharging all expenses, together with the nurse's and physicians' bills, PAID HER THE FULL AMOUNT OF HER WAGES FOR THE WHOLE TIME, as if she had always been in actual service.

It is always delightful to record, and to dwell upon, an instance of real generosity; and the single example of this excellent lady is worth folios of theory on this subject; for it comes home to the heart with the sweetest teachings of that charity, which is the very essence of the christian character; and, without which, indeed, to use the beautiful language of Paul:—"Though I speak as with the tongue of man, and of angels, I am become as sounding brass or a tinkling cymbal. And though I had the gift of prophecy, and understood all mysteries, and all knowledge; and though I have all faith so that I could remove mountains, and have not CHARITY, I am nothing."

Pleasant as the perfume distilled from roses, and indestructible as the purest gold, will be the memory of Jane C——; for it shall be written in the bosoms of many, and inscribed in burnished characters on the brightening tablet of Humanity. The very existence of disinterested benevolence has been made a doubt; but, with such instances in view, human nature feels itself exalted, and begins to learn its own divinity. Statues of brass shall perish and be forgotten; but the principles of goodness shall be caught from heart to heart, through countless generations; still living, and still blessing, age after age, undying as their ETERNAL SOURCE.

From the time when she was taken sick, it was three months before Elleanor could recommence her business. On her return to Providence she went to Miss C—'s father's, where she remained a week, being treated with the kindest attention. She then went to Warwick, where she staid until her health was so far reestablished as to admit of her commencing work; when she returned to Providence and resumed her accustomed routine of business.

Notwithstanding the great kindness of Miss C——, Elleanor refused to go out to New York to live with her the succeeding winter; for she was afraid of being again sick, and subjecting her kind mistress to a new succession of troubles. The next winter, accordingly, she staid in town; and worked at Mr. Mathewson's for two dollars a week. At this place Elleanor was so well contented, that she lived there the succeeding winter. Then she went to Mr. Davis Dyer's, a small and very pleasant family. And here, dear reader, let us wait for the beginning of the next chapter.

CHAPTER VIII.

I should have mentioned before, that about sixteen years ago, Elleanor, having six hundred dollars on hand, bought a lot, for which she paid one hundred dollars, all in silver money, as she has herself assured me. She then commenced building a house, which cost seventeen hundred dollars. This house was all paid for, with no encumbrance whatever. After it had been built three or four years; she built an addition on the east side, to live in herself; and subsequently one on the west side, to accommodate an additional tenant. This house rented for one hundred and fifty dollars per annum.—About this time there were two lots of land for sale, of which Elleanor wished to become the purchaser. Not having money enough she hired of a gentleman of Warwick, two hundred and forty dollars. For this she was to pay interest at the rate of ten per cent; and, by agreement, so long as she could do so, she might be entitled to keep the money; i.e. she was to pay the interest, and renew the note annually.

Elleanor had completed her house, which with its two wings, and its four chimneys, wore quite an imposing aspect; and in the honest pride and joy of her heart, she looked upon it with delight; as well she might do, since it was all earned by her own honest labors, and afforded the prospect of a happy home, and a comfortable income in her old age. Attached to this house, and belonging to a Mrs. —— was a gangway which Elleanor wished very much to obtain possession of, as she was entirely cut off from out door privileges, without it. She had hired it for five years; and had often spoken to Mrs. —— in regard to the purchase.

But what was her surprise to find, that just before the term of her lease had expired, Mrs. —— had sold it. Mr. C—— then, who owned the house and premises adjoining her own, came directly forward and offered to sell to Elleanor, and as she felt very anxious to secure the privilege of the gang-way, she finally determined to do so; although, by doing so, she was obliged to involve herself considerably. This house had been built by Mr. C——, who, being unable to pay for it, had given a mortgage of the premises. At this time Elleanor had five hundred dollars in her possession, which she had been wishing to dispose of to the best advantage. She finally came to a bargain with Mr. C——, agreeing to give two thousand dollars for the house. She paid the five hundred dollars down; and then gave a mortgage on the house to Mr. Greenold, for fifteen hundred dollars. This was to be paid in four years; which, if she had received the least indulgence, she might easily have done; or rather if she had not, in her own honesty of heart, been led to confide in the PROMISE of ONE, who had more regard for his PURSE, than for his HONOR, or his CHRISTIAN CHARACTER, as we shall soon see.

In September, 1831, Elleanor was again seized with the typhus fever, which left her in so low a state of health, that her friends and herself, feared she was falling into a decline. With a strong impression of this feeling upon her mind, she wished much to see her friends in Massachusetts again; and finally she persuaded her brother to accompany her on a journey thither.

She went out to Warwick, and remained there six weeks, until she believed she had regained her health, so far as to undertake the journey; when she returned to Providence, and, with her brother George, made arrangements for her departure. Accordingly, in October, Elleanor having left all her affairs in a good train, with her brother, sat off for Adams.

For the first day she seemed somewhat invigorated with the ride, and the change of air and scene; but the unusual fatigue on the second and third days, quite overcame her.

They stopped for the night at Angell's tavern, in Hadley, where Elleanor found herself very ill. In the morning, her brother, finding she did not rise, tapped on her chamber door, and asked her if she felt well enough to pursue her journey. She replied that she was sick, and could not go any further that day. Her brother went to the land-lady, and requested permission to remain through the day, as his sister was too ill to proceed. From this circumstance—this trifling fact—sprang all the subsequent troubles of Elleanor. It so happened that there were two persons from Providence, within the hearing of George Eldridge, when he made the above named request; and as they had some knowledge of his sister, they made their report, when they returned to Providence. This, she being very sick, like a gathering snow-ball, grew as it went the rounds of gossip, into exceedingly dangerous illness—the point of death; and finally by the simple process of accumulation, it was resolved into death itself. Who could have foreseen results so disastrous as those which followed, could have been occasioned by such a trifle. The reader will subsequently find, how all Elleanor's troubles sprang from the wanton carelessness of those, who so busily circulated the story of her death.

"What mighty oaks from little acorns grow."
and, what a lesson of caution should be drawn from this simple fact, and its consequences.—How careful ought we to be to speak nothing but the truth, even in regard to the most trifling circumstances; and not only so, but to be well assured that what we suppose to be true, is TRUTH, before we receive it as such.

CHAPTER IX.

After resting a day Elleanor was able to continue her journey; and she arrived at its end without accident, or further difficulty, though considerably fatigued.

She found her friends all well, and delighted to see her once more. It soon came to pass that the eye of George Eldridge, rested with a very pointed expression of kindness on his cousin, Miss Ruth Jacobs, whom we have before had occasion to notice, as being the confidential friend of Elleanor. George Eldridge had been unhappy in a former matrimonial connection; and this circumstance heightened the interest which his sister felt in this second affair. Being anxious to promote it to the utmost, she yielded to his wishes, and consented to remain in Adams through the winter. Her brother soon found business at wood-cutting; and found also, what was better, that the gentle eye of his cousin Ruth, could, by no means, look coldly upon him. This last, indeed, soon became no secret. The proposals were duly made, and frankly accepted; so the winter passed away, cheerily and happily, Elleanor spending the time among her numerous relations.

But when spring came, Elleanor's thoughts began to turn homeward. Her brother, however, shewed himself in no haste to quit the pleasant orbit of the amiable Ruth. But having been invited by Elleanor to accompany her home, Ruth determined to make a visit to R. Island; so, as they took the magnet along with them, there was no further difficulty. George Eldridge, with no inconsiderable degree of pride, seated himself between his sister and cousin Ruth, and turned towards home. Their journey thither was cheered by fine weather and pleasant chat;

and all were happy; for the Janus, Fortune, had not shown her evil face to Elleanor.

On the evening of the third day they arrived at Elleanor's house, in Providence; and, after having laid off her travelling dress, our heroine prepared for supper.

It was just at dusk when she ran across the street for bread. She stepped in at the door, as usual, and asked for bread. But the baker's boy, instead of supplying her, ran back into the entry, with an appearance of great alarm; and, having stood gazing at her a moment, with his arms extended in a horizontal line, and mouth and eyes laid open to their full extent, with the most querulous and misgiving tones, he called out: "Is that you Ellen?—Why I thought you was—dead!"

"No; I am not dead;" replied Ellenor, "but I am hungry. Give me some bread, quick!"—and, supposing the boy was trying to hoax her, she stepped forward as she spoke.

The boy still retreated, and still holding out his hands, as if to ward off danger, he cried out: "Don't come any nearer!—don't Ellen, if you *be* Ellen—cause—cause—I don't like dead folks!"

It was some time before Elleanor could assure the poor little fellow of her real, *bona fide* bodily presence, so strongly was he impressed with the belief that she was actually "departed." Her appearance too, coming in as she did, unannounced, at the dim, uncertain hour of twilight, must have had, to his excited imagination, something really terrible in it. Had the boy reflected a moment, he would have seen that it was out of all rule, and entirely without precedent, for a ghost to cry for bread; but Jamie, like many of his species, was no philosopher.

This was the first that Elleanor knew of the story of her death; though she heard of it repeatedly during the evening, and the next morning. Her brother heard also at the hotel, where he went to put up his horse, that his sister's property had been attached, and was advertised to be sold, in consequence of a report concerning her death; but he did not mention it to Elleanor that evening, knowing her to be very much fatigued; and, as he expected to take her directly out to Warwick the next day, it seemed unnecessary; for then, and not till then, would she be able to see the gentleman; and, as he hoped, make some arrangements with him.—However, the time was not long before she heard of it; and, of course, she felt very disagreeably.

Two of their cousins, Jeremiah and Lucy Prophet, went out to War-wick with them; and they had anticipated a joyful occasion, on the arrival, and introduction, of the bride-elect; but poor Ellen's trouble cast a damp upon the whole party.

As soon as the news of their arrival had gone about, the gentleman who had laid an attachment on Ellen's property, in order to procure the liquidation of the two hundred and forty dollar note before alluded to, came directly to see her; and that too altogether of his own accord. This gentleman was not the original creditor; who had deceased, leaving his brother as his sole heir.

The gentleman told Ellen what he had done; at the same time saying, that he should never have done it, had he not been told that she was dead. "But," said he, "I am glad you have returned, safe and well; and though I want the money, I WILL NEVER DISTRESS YOU FOR IT."

Ellen had the simplicity to believe this, because the man—perhaps I ought to say GENTLEMAN—was a member of a church; and was CALLED a christian. Poor, simple-hearted, honest Ellen: she did not know then that she had met "the wolf in sheep's clothing!"

The above promise was given at the house of George Eldridge, in the presence of him, Ruth Jacobs, Jeremiah, and Lucy Prophet.—After Mr. —— had gone, these all spoke of his promise one to another, bid-ding Ellen be of good courage, as she could now have nothing to fear. THEY, also, it seems, were so very simple as to understand the gentle-man's words as a promise, though probably HE intended them as only an expression of COURTESY.

I remember an anecdote, which though simple, is "a case in point." A gentleman who had removed to the country, had for his neighbor a Frenchman, who had the national characteristic of exceeding polite-ness. The gentleman kept no horse; and, as he took frequent walks about the country, his polite neighbor always remonstrated with him, in strong terms, begging that he would make him so very happy, as to use his horse—ALWAYS. This offer was so often repeated, that, at length, the gentleman determined he would avail himself of his neighbor's generosity; so one day he told him he should be very glad to have the loan of his horse, for a short ride.

"By no means;" replied the Frenchman.—"I have but von horse; an' him I vant—"

"But you have repeatedly offered him to me."

"Ah! my dear neighbor," replied the Frenchman, with a very significant and sweet smile, "you's be MOST WELCOME TO DE COMPLIMEN."

How much of that which assumes to be kindness, could it be
reduced to its true analysis, would be found simply "A WELCOME TO
THE COMPLIMENT."

CHAPTER X.

Elleanor had given Mr. —— a conditional promise that she would raise a hundred dollars for him in April; but it so happened that she could not procure the money; and, relying on his promise of indulgence, which his his honor as a gentleman, and his christian character, alike conspired to strengthen; while, at the same time, his great wealth, or entire independence, placed him altogether above any temptation to uncharitableness.

In about a week she returned to Providence, satisfied that, in the withdrawal of his suit, Mr. —— had fairly "buried the hatchet," she commenced her summer's work with renewed vigor. This was the cholera season, which brought so much of terror with it, as to be long remembered. Ellen's usual business was somewhat modified by the prevailing sickness; and being a skillful and fearless person, she went much among the sick; and by her zealous attentions to the wants of the suffering, she won the kindest regard of all who were so fortunate as to obtain her valuable services.

In August Mrs. T——, having a daughter who was pronounced to be either afflicted with, or liable to, the cholera, left town for her country residence, in Pomfret, Connecticut. She engaged Elleanor to accompany her in the capacity of nurse and attendant.

In order to make all secure before leaving town, Ellen paid up all that was due on the mortgage: but she did not pay Mr. —— because she could not do so without great loss, and difficulty; and concerning this she felt no uneasiness, because there had been an express understanding between herself and the deceased Mr. ——, that she should have the money so long as she could pay the interest of ten per cent on the note: and besides her well-known character for integrity and industry, seemed to secure the promise of indulgence, which had been voluntarily given.

Ellen's last step was to go round among her families, and request them to be careful and prudent in all things, making no disturbance, and committing no trespass: and she assured them that if she heard any complaint from her neighbors, she should turn out the offenders, as soon as she returned.

Intent only upon her new duties, Elleanor then entered zealously into the service of Mrs. T.; and with that lady, and her family, left town for Pomfret, a distance of only thirty miles. The sickness of Mrs. T. and that of her family, rendered our heroine's activity and skill of peculiar value.

In about two months, the family of Mrs. T. having recovered, and the cholera panic having somewhat subsided, that lady determined to return to Providence. On arriving in the city, she stopped at the Franklin House, still retaining Ellen in attendance. The next morning after their arrival, a lady came in and told Mrs. T.—that the property of Elleanor was all attached, and sold; and to the latter, the sad intelligence was speedily announced; but she found it very difficult to believe a story, at once, so entirely opposed to all her convictions of right, and so fraught with distress and anguish to herself; yet, upon enquiry, she found that one half the truth had not been told.

Mr. ——, of Warwick, had attached and sold property, which a few months before had been valued at four thousand dollars, for the pitiful sum of two hundred and forty dollars.—Why he wished to attach so large a property, for so small a debt, is surprising enough; since Elleanor had then in her possession two house lots, and the little house and lot at Warwick; either of which would have been snfficient to liquidate the debt. There seems to be a spirit of wilful malignity, in this wanton destruction of property, which it is difficult to conceive of as existing in the bosom of civilized man.

One after another, all the aggravating particulars came to the knowledge and notice of Ellen. In the first place, the attachment, as we have before said, was entirely disproportioned to the debt; which the general good character, integrity, and PROPERTY of the debtor, rendered perfectly secure. In the second place, the sheriff never legally advertised the sale, or advertised it all, as can be learned. In the third place, the auctioneer, having, doubtless, ascertained the comfortable fact, that the owner was a laboring colored woman, who was then away, leaving no friend to protect her rights, struck it off, almost at the first bid; and at little more than one third its value; it being sold for only fifteen hundred dollars, which was the exact amount of the mortgage. In the fourth place, the purchaser, after seeing the wrongfulness of the whole affair, and after giving his word three successive times, that he would settle and restore the property for a given sum, twice meanly flew from his bargain, successively making larger demands. "Is not this a heinous crime; yea, an iniquity to be punished by the judges;" yet the chief actors in this affair, were all good and "HONORABLE men!" They shall learn that "He that loveth silver shall not be satisfied with silver; nor he that loveth abundance, with increase."* They shall find that, "As a partridge sitteth on eggs, and hatcheth them not, so he that getteth riches, and not by RIGHT, shall leave them in the midst of his days:"† and "Men shall clap their hands at him, and hiss him out of his place."‡

* Ecclesiastes, v. 10.
† Jeremiah, xvii. 11,
‡ Job, xxvii. 23.

CHAPTER XII.[*]

Thus, as we have seen, was Ellen, in a single moment, by a single stroke of the hammer, deprived of the fruits of all her honest and severe labors—the labors of years; and, not only so, but actually thrown in debt for many small bills, for repairs and alterations on her houses, which she had the honor and honesty to discharge, even against the advices of some of her friends, after the property by which they had been incurred had been so cruelly taken away. Elleanor has traits of character, which, if she were a white woman, would be called NOBLE. And must color so modify character, that they are not still so?

On visiting the premises, sad, indeed was the sight which the late owner witnessed. The two wings of her first house, which she had herself built, with their chimneys, had been pulled down: and it seemed as if the spirit of Ruin had been walking abroad. All her families had been compelled to leave, at a single week's notice; and many of them, being unable to procure tenements, were compelled to find shelter in barns and out-houses, or even in the woods. But THEY WERE COLORED PEOPLE—So thought he, who so unceremoniously ejected them from their comfortable homes; and he is not only a PROFESSED friend to their race, but "AN HONORABLE MAN."

Let us return to the point where we left our story, and our heroine, at the Franklin House. Mrs. T. kindly furnished Ellen with her horse and

---

* The original 1838 edition of *Memoirs* misnumbered Chapters 11 and 12 as Chapters 12 and 13. No text seems to be missing from either the original edition nor from the present reprint. [Moody, Ed.]

chaise and advised her to go directly to Warwick, to see the gentleman on whose promise she had so confidently relied.

Mark his excuse. How noble—how manly it was! He told Ellen he was very sorry for what he had done; but that he never should have done it, *if the lawyer had not advised him to.* He must have been a man of stern principle—of sterling independence, to perpetrate such an act, *because his lawyer advised him to.* I pity the man whose invention is so poor—so miserable, that he could not fabricate a better falsehood. "Wo unto them that decree unrighteous decrees, and that write grievances which they have prescribed, to TURN ASIDE THE NEEDY FROM JUDGEMENT and to TAKE AWAY THE RIGHT FROM THE POOR OF MY PEOPLE, that widows may be their prey, and they may ROB THE FATHERLESS. What will ye do in the day of visitation, and in the desolation which shall come from far? To whom will ye flee for help, and where will ye leave your glory?"*

After a time, a ray of hope dawned on the dark path of Ellen. She consulted Mr. Greene, the State's attorney, and found that she might bring forward a case of "Trespass and Ejectment," against the purchaser of her property. She had hope to repudiate the whole sale and purchase, on the ground of the illegal or non-advertisement of the sale. This case was brought before the Court of Common Pleas, in January, 1837.

Of course, the whole success of it turned on the point of the sheriff's oath, in regard to the advertisement. When the oath was administered, the sheriff appeared strangely agitated, and many, then present in court, even the judge, thought it was the perturbation of guilt. Nevertheless he attested upon oath, that he had put up the notification in three public places;—viz. at Manchester's tavern bar-room, on the Court-house door in time of Court, and on Market square. There were three men who came prepared to take their oath, that the notice was never put up at Manchester's; thus invalidating that part of his testimony; but it was found that the oaths of common men could not be taken against that of the High Sheriff. So the case was decided against the plaintiff.

Ellen's next step was to hire two men, whom she fee'd liberally, to make enquiries throughout the city, in regard to those notifications.— They went about, two days, making all possible search for light in

---

* Isaiah, x. 1, 2, 3.

regard to the contested notifications, calling upon all those who frequented public places. But no person could be found, who had either seen them, or heard of their being seen. A fine advertisement, truly! And here, let me ask, why was not this sale advertised in the public papers? The same answer that has been given before, will suffice now. THE OWNER OF THE PROPERTY WAS A LABORING COLORED WOMAN. Is not this reply, TRUTH as it is, a LIBEL on the character of those who wrought the work of evil?

Elleanor then brought an action against the sheriff, tending to destroy his testimony in the late case; and on the very day when it was to be laid before the court, Mr. ———, the purchaser, came forward and told Ellen's attorney, that he would restore the property for twenty-one hundred dollars, and two years' rent. Ellen then withdrew her case, and set herself about procuring the money. This she raised; and it was duly tendered to Mr. ———. But mark HIS regard for his word. He then said that Ellen had been so long* in procuring the money, that he must have twenty-three hundred dollars.

The additional two hundred dollars were then raised, but the gentleman, in consequence of repairs and alterations, which he could have had no right to make, and require pay for, as the case stood, next demanded twenty-five hundred dollars, with six months' rent.

The suspended action had, in the mean time, been again brought forward; and was to have been tried before the Circuit Court. But so anxious was Ellen again to possess the property, that she once more withdrew her action, and came to the exorbitant terms of Mr. ———. She again hired the additional two hundred dollars; and finally effected a settlement.

This conduct, on the part of the purchaser, requires no comment; for its meanness, not to say dishonesty, is self-evident in the simplest statement of the facts themselves. But this is not all. The sheriff had informed Mr. ———, that he could sue Elleanor for house rent, as her goods had never been removed from the tenement she had occupied.

---

* She had great difficulty in obtaining it, as it was then the period of the greatest pressure; and it was next to impossible to get money at all. That Elleanor was able to procure twenty-one hundred dollars, upon her own credit, at such a time, in the space of six weeks, of itself shews the esteem in which she was held, as well as the energy and perseverance, for which she has always been remarkable.

This he actually did, and laid an attachment on her furniture, which was advertised to be sold at public auction: and it would have been, had not a gentleman who had the management of her business, gone forward and settled with Mr. ——.

The whole affair, from beginning to end, in all its connections and bearings, was A WEB OF INIQUITY. It was a wanton outrage upon the simplest and most evident principles of justice. But the subject of this wrong, or rather of this accumulation of wrongs, was a woman, and therefore weak—a COLORED WOMAN—and therefore contemptible. No MAN ever would have been treated so; and if A WHITE WOMAN had been the subject of such wrongs, the whole town—nay, the whole country, would have been indignant: and the actors would have been held up to the contempt they deserve!—The story would have flown upon the wings of the wind to the most remote borders of our land. Newspaper editors would have copied, and commented on it, till every spirit of honor, of justice, and of chivalry, would have been roused. At home benevolent SOCIETIES would have met, and taken efficient means to relieve the sufferer; while every heart would have melted in kindness, and every bosom have poured out its sympathy. Is this wrong the less a wrong, because the subject of it is weak and defenceless? By the common laws of HONOR, it is cowardice to strike the unarmed and the weak. By the same rule, HE WHO INJURES THE DEFENCELESS, ADDS MEANNESS TO CRIME.

Let us look more fully into the merits of this case; and enquire how far Elleanor is entitled to the sympathies, and the charities of the humane. She has been industrious, and persevering in all her labors. Her moral character stands without reproach, fair as the fairest cheek of beauty. Though earnest and successful in the acquisition of money, she is not miserly, or parsimonious, when any kindness is called for, or good work is to be done. She gives freely to those who need; both to individuals, and societies. She subscribes for papers which she cannot read, in order to promote the circulation of truth, whether moral, or religious. Her losses are to be attributed, mainly,*

---

* One of the chief causes, was her reliance upon what she considered THE WORD OF HONOR, of the Warwick gentleman; for, had she believed it *necessary*, she could have raised the money, without a doubt.

to a want of knowledge in business, by which she became a prey to the wanton carelessness, if not the willful and deliberate wickedness, of men, who SHOULD have been the very last to have seized the spoils of the weak.

Are there none to feel for her? Are there none to sustain, and encourage her? Thank God!—there are already a few—a few benevolent, and noble-minded women, who dare come forward and publicly DEFEND THE RIGHT, and DENOUNCE THE WRONG. May the bright and living spark of LOVE, which illumines their bosoms, kindle and expand itself, until, flying from heart to heart, and from soul to soul, all the friends of humanity will catch the sacred flame. It is pleasant to do good. The very act of generosity is its own reward. Then will not every reader of this little book, recommend it to the notice of the humane, and endeavor to promote its sale; not for its own sake, but for the sake of her, who depends upon its success, for deliverance from the difficulties in which she is involved. Ellen has yet a large debt to liquidate, before her estate is freed from its incumbrance. With a little timely help, together with her earnings, she may be able to do this.

The compiler of these memoirs feels bound to confess, that they are brought before the public in a very imperfect manner; but if their SUCCESS is proportioned to the earnest and zealous WISHES of the writer, poor Elleanor will have cause to rejoice. Inelegances and inaccuracies of style and language, are unavoidable necessities in the case; and if any are disposed to find fault with the author's poor labor, let him remember that it was not undertaken for the desire of fame, or the love of money, but with the sole and single hope, of DOING GOOD. There is no personal animosity, on the writer's part, to any to whom allusions may have been made. No names, in such cases, have been used; and if *notorious fact* lay not bare the bosom, nor *conscience* strike home the knife, there will be no reproach, and no wound.

And TO WHOMSOVER IT MAY CONERN, I will say: "Seek ye out the Book of the Lord, and read."

"Whatsoever ye would that men should do to you, do ye even so unto them."

"Pure religion, and undefiled before God and the Father, is this; To visit the fatherless and the widow, in their affliction, and to keep UNSPOTTED FROM THE WORLD."

"Thus saith the Lord God; surely, because my flock became a prey, and my flock became meat to every beast of the field, because there was no shepherd, neither did my shepherds search for my flock; but the shepherds fed themselves; Therefore, O, ye shepherds! hear the word of the Lord. Thus saith the Lord God; Behold I am against the shepherds; and I will require my flock at their hands; neither shall the shepherds FEED THEMSELVES any more; for I will deliver my flock from their mouth, that they be no more meat for them."†

"Who shall ascend into the Hill of the Lord and who shall stand in his holy place? He that hath clean hands and a pure heart who hath not lifted up his soul unto vanity, nor SWORN DECEITFULLY."‡

"Let no man say when he is tempted, I am tempted of God; for God cannot be tempted of evil; neither tempteth he any man."§

"Whoso KEEPETH HIS WORD, in him, verily, is the love of God perfected."

"Thou hast sent widows away empty; and THE ARMS OF THE FATHERLESS HAVE BEEN BROKEN; for thou hast taken a pledge of thy brother for nought, and stripped the naked of his clothing."

"Neither thieves, nor COVETOUS, nor revilers, nor EXTORTIONERS, shall inherit the kingdom of God."

Of course, the edge and point of these quotations, will be determined by individual circumstances. But they were spoken by the inspiration of Him, who is a God of justice, and by whom "ACTIONS are weighed."

---

* James 1, 27,
† Exekiel 34, 8, 9, 10.
‡ Psalms 24, 3, 4.
§ James 1, 13.

CHAPTER XIII.

Since writing the above, a passage in the life of Elleanor has come to my knowledge, which, I think, deserves particular notice; since it affords a happy illustration of one trait in her character, that of generosity, and noble self-sacrifice to the welfare of friends. It happened that her brother Geore Eldridge some time in the April of 1832, was for an alleged crime, arrested and thrown into prison. He was accused of having horse-whipped, and of otherwise barbarously treating a man upon the highway. As soon as the report came to the knowledge of Elleanor, she determined to liberate him, at all hazards; because she felt assured, from all his previous course of conduct, and from his well-established character and habits, that he could not be guilty of the offence with which he was charged.

These views of Elleanor were strongly opposed by her friends, who feared she might involve herself in some dificulty, and advised her to have nothing to do with the matter. But these objections could not satisfy such a mind as Elleanor's; and obeying alone the dictates of humanity, benevolence, and natural love, she generously committed herself to the guardianship of her brother's rights. This brother had a wife and family; and the consequence of being detained in prison, for six months, as he must have been, to await his trial in the spring, would have been, not only unpleasant, but distressing. Elleanor could allow of no such thing; for, of what use would her property be, if it could not purchase for her, the smallest of all luxuries, that of relieving the distress of a friend?

Being at once resolved, she sent to a livery stable for the handsomest horse and chaise it afforded; for Ellen was determined to go in a style accordant with the dignity of her mission. On arriving at the Greenwich gaol, she found her brother in a state of great distress, in view of his long imprisonment, and the consequent affliction and suffering of his family. How delightful then to Ellen, was the consciousness of power to relieve him! Was there any thing in the abstract possession of money, houses, or lands, that could, for one moment, be weighed against it? She thought not.

The business was soon settled. Elleanor gave bonds for five hundred dollars; liberated her brother, and took upon herself the whole management of his case.

The October following it was to have been brought forward; but, on account of the absence of some important witnesses, the defendant prayed that it might be continued to the spring term, the following April; which was granted. The trial was then suspended again on account of the illness of the defendant's advocate: and, finally, was tried the next October term; when the accused was honorably acquitted; as nothing could be proved against him, while, on the contrary, he was able to establish his entire innocence, by the fullest and clearest evidence. Elleanor managed this case entirely; and, on account of it, was subjected to considerable cost and trouble; but she never regretted having engaged in it, and would freely have expended much more, had it been necessary to effect her purpose.

This was the first law suit in which our heroine has been engaged. She has since managed one for herself; yet not with equal success; and, with this experience in the law, she declares herself fully satisfied; and she has no desire to enter its mazes again.

Some of our young and romantic readers, may feel curious to know why Elleanor never married. When questioned on the subject, she says that she has determined to profit by the advice of her aunt, who told her never to marry, because it involved such A WASTE OF TIME; for, said she, "while my young mistress was courting and marrying, I knit five pairs of stockings." This is the reply that Ellen generally gives; but as she has had several good offers, WE can look back to the records of the past, and think of a tenderer, and deeper reason.

But we must now give to the subject of these memories a parting blessing. Be not discouraged. All will yet be well. Is there not a voice of hope and peace, whispering within thee, "I have seen thy tears behold I will heal thee," "I will seek that which was lost; I will bind up that which was broken, and will* strengthen that which was sick."† Thou shalt, indeed, escape "as a bird out of the snare of the fowlers; for the snare is broken. Though thou hast eaten the bread of adversity, and drunk the waters of affliction, let thy soul be staid upon his promises," of whom it is said: "He shall deliver thee in six troubles; yea, in seven shall no evil touch thee."‡ He who disappointeth the designs of the crafty, shall lead thee forth beside the still waters of peace; and into thy grateful heart shall be poured the song of joy. How pleasant will be the sound of thy rejoicing, when it finds an echo in the heart of thy kind protectresses.

"Be strong and be of good courage; fear not, nor be afraid; for the Lord thy God, he it is that doth go with thee; he will not fail thee nor forsake thee."§

And for all thy wrongs and sufferings, mayst thou reap blessings a hundred fold.

---

* 2 Kings 20, 5.
† Ezekial 34, 16.
‡ Job 5, 19
§ Deuteronomy 31, 6.

APPENDIX.

―――――

The following pieces were handed to Elleanor, to publish in her book, as testimonies of the kind regard, and earnest wishes for her success, of the several ladies who presented them. And first we have an

APPEAL TO STRANGERS—
In behalf of the subject of the Narrative contained in this book.

To purchase it in compassion and kindness to a stranger in distress, whose only hope rests on its sale, you are earnestly solicited. Your charity I trust will be rewarded by an approving heart, should you learn at a future, and perhaps not far distant day, that your liberal and willing hands have saved a human being, deserving a better fate, from poverty and distress. To those who know Elleanor an appeal is unnecessary— they have generously subscribed for this work. But this alone will not relieve her, as the expenses of printing, binding, &c., must be paid out of their subscription. Therefore, on strangers rests her only hope of worldly comfort. Let her not be disappointed, for the trifling sum she asks of each. Finally, in the words of scripture, "Execute ye judgment and righteousness; and deliver the spoiled out of the hands of the oppressor."

―――――

Next we find a piece written by a little girl. It brings to notice one trait of Ellen's character, that of unwearying kindness to children, which never fails to win their innocent little hearts, and fill them with the warmest love.

I write these few lines as a testimony of my good wishes for the welfare of Elleanor Eldridge, who worked, from time to time, in my father's family, long before, and ever since, I entered into life. She was always considered in our family as praise-worthy, for her good conduct, industry, and economy, as well as for her temperance and virtue. She may be considered as a *pattern of morality*, making no mockery of religion, which she never experienced. I never heard her make use of unbecoming words, or speak ill of any person. She would not have been so liable to impositions in the transaction of business, which were the original cause of the loss of her property, if she had been favored with a good education in early life, which, in mature years, she in vain endeavored to acquire. On the other hand if she had received an early education, her mind might have soared above a laborious life, and her useful labors lost to the world.* As what is past cannot be recalled, I hope the public in pity for her misfortunes will liberally subscribe for the history of her life.

M. W.

Here comes a scrap of poety to enliven us after the dull and uniform march of prose.

---

* This is rather an old fashioned sentiment. My kind little cousin will learn, one of these days, that education, instead of unfitting a person for the useful and necessary occupations of life, acts upon the mind as a DISCIPLINE, teaching it to sustain and strengthen itself, not only against the most heavy trials; but the most severe labors; so that the harder the lot, the greater would be the actual necessity of education. When all are educated—and, sooner or later, all must be—no honest occupation will be degrading: and the humblest pursuits will be invested with new dignity, while each one labors in the calling to which he is appointed.—Ed. [Whipple herself is the Editor referenced in the appendices; C. R. Williams is "the writer."]

THE AFRICAN'S APPEAL.

Why rejected? wherefore base?
Is our long degraded race?
Are we not of human kind?
Have we not the gift of mind?
Which learning can and doth improve,
A heart to feel! a heart to love.
And what's tincture of the skin?
If all is pure and fair within.
It is the beauty of the MIND,
Pure and holy and refined,
That can raise the soul above
Earthborn cares, to Heaven above.
And must that culture be denied?
And must we toil to pampered pride?
And shall our hard earned labors fail,
And white men our dear rights assail?
Forbid it all the powers above!
Forbit it, Oh, thou God of Love.

E. C. J.

HARD FATE OF POOR ELLEN.

BY A LADY OF PROVIDENCE.

The weary day had sunk to rest,
    Nature lay hushed in soft repose;
Evening rolled on, in sable vest—
    The moon in dewy stillness rose.

Silent, I sat in musing mood,
    Reflecting on frail life's short date;
Among mankind how few were good—
    For wealth, what strife, and fierce debate.

A deep-drawn sign fell on my ear;
    A slow step lingered at my door—
I cried, "Come in,—you need not fear,"
    To a lone female, sad and poor.

She said she'd labored *thirty years*,
    In servile toil, had spent her prime—
Through grief and care, and sweat, and tears,
    To save against a needy time.

Of comforts, she, herself denied,—
    Hoping, in time, to have a home;
All her hard earnings, laid aside,
    At length, the joyful time had come.—

A house and home, were now here own;
    By honest industry, 'twas reared;
She dreamed of happiness, alone—
    She knew no foes, no *fraud*, she feared.

But, too secure, in evil hour—
    The wily snare, for her, was laid,
Her absence, gave it *legal* power,
    Her home was seized, and she betrayed!

Poor colored Ellen! now bereft
    Of all on earth, she called her own;
Nought, but honest HEART, is left,
    To struggle in her grief alone.

Where is the man, could be so base—
    Against the helpless and forlorn?
Let him, forever, hide his face!
    If he would shun *deserved scorn*.

Sweet sympathy! O, shed one tear!
    Humanity! pray lend your aid;
And, if you're not rewarded *here*,—
    In *heaven*, you will be *over-paid*.

S. P.

TO THE PUBLIC,

"The Poor," said our Saviour, "we have always with us." While the situation and the wrongs of the distant Indian, and the Southern slave, is exciting so much commisseration, we ought not to lose sight of the oppressed and afflicted in our own immediate vicinity. The situation of poor Ellen, robbed of all her hard-earned property, by the chicanery of the law, is worthy of all compassion. To her moral character Ellen can bring the best of testimonials; and of her industry, enterprize, and untiring perseverance, in accumulating and husbanding her property, there is most incontrovertible proof.

It has been the constant complaint of all disposed to withhold aid to any of her color, that they are constitutionally and wilfully indolent, and averse to any kind of labor—that they are not absolutely driven to; but surely no such complaint can be made of the subject of this Narrative. She had by unceasing application, in her humble and laborious employments, got together a sum sufficient to build her a house,* with the exception of a small sum, which her industry would in a few years have enabled her to repay, where she borrowed it. But the remorseless creditor waits not for the debtor to be enabled to repay, but for the moment when under the shadow of the law, he may snatch all. This poor woman, ignorant of the technicalities and sinuosities of the law, reposed in the vain confidence, that others would be guided by the sense of justice, that she had imbibed herself; nor dreamed but that law and justice would go hand in hand. From this dream, however, she was compelled to awake, and find herself stripped of her property: The blow must have been dreadful, and to many, would have operated as a check to all further effort. Yet we see she does not despond; her reliance in Providence is not withdrawn, but knowing that Providence acts by means; and those means most generally, through the instrumentality of individual exertion, she is again preparing to renew her efforts. Whether this effort is to be crowned with success, remains with the public. Fifty cents is not great for any individual to bestow, and it is very sincerely hoped by the writer of this article, that the humble memoirs

---

* The writer is laboring under a slight mistake. Elleanor had already built and PAID FOR one house in this city, besides her house in Warwick. It was the purchase of a second house which involved her.—ED.

of the unfortunate and persevering woman who is the subject of this narrative will meet with a ready sale.

It is worthy of consideration, that if Ellen, with her limited improvements, and under all the disadvantages of colour, could achieve so much as she has, what she would have done if those disadvantages had not been in the way.

Finally, in befriending Ellen, we have the pleasure of assisting one who carries in her veins not only the blood of some of the Aborigines of our own State (the unfortunate and extinct race of the warlike Pequots)' but of that much wronged and abused people, who have been sold into slavery on our Coasts, and although charity ought not to *expend itself* upon one subject, it is our opinion that it ought to begin in our neighborhood, and be exercised on those who come in our way before those who are at more remote distance, and who will not be in the way to be benefitted by our sympathies.

C. R. WILLIAMS.

Providence, October 19th, 1838.

TO ELLEN.

As God, in his providence, has put it into the hearts of some of your good friends, to publish a book, giving an account of your trials, and sufferings, in this vale of tears; trials which if rightly improved by you, and sanctified to you, will make you rich, in the kingdom of glory— rich in the enjoyment of those *durable riches,* which can never be *wrested* from your grasp, by the hand of the covetous man, nor oppressor. For you find by painful experience, that the *riches of this world,* take to themselves wings, and flee away. And that there is "nothing true *but heaven,*" For the heart of man is deceitful above all things. When you

---

' Probably Mrs. W. meant to say the Narragansetts.—The territory of the Pequot tribe lay chiefly in Connecticut. But Elleanor is descended from the noble race of Canonicus and Miantonomo, who were for a long time, the generous protectors and friends of Roger Williams.—HER fore-fathers, then, nourished and protected OURS. ED.

most needed the hand of brotherly kindness extended towards you, and expected the words of friendship and affection from those who have professed humanity and friendship and love for your race, professing to teach them how to enjoy the rights and privileges which an Indulgent Father has so richly lavished upon all his creatures, without regard to grade or color, you have been cruelly deceived even by those who have bowed themselves before the Altar of God, to supplicate the divine benediction upon you, and to pray that the heart of the oppressor may be melted and the oppressed be suffered to go free. Have they not practically denied their faith, tempting the God of Heaven by their hypocrisy? I doubt not when you see this, you are ready to exclaim, there is no confidence in the flesh. But judge not of the blessed religion of Jesus, by the conduct of those who have proved recreant to their trust, for *pure religion*, is that which will pity the Fartherless, in their affliction, and labor to retrieve, the wrongs done to the Orphan.

But, in coming before the world to make known your trials, you find that mankind are not all alike, that there are hearts, that beat warm with sympathy for their fellow beings, and breasts that "the milk of human-kindness" hath warmed with love, and tenderness for abused innocence. But labor, my friend, to make a *practical improvement*, of these afflictions, and make him your friend, that "sticketh closer than a brother." Then, when trials press heavy, and friends forsake; when riches fade away, you may safely say, I know in whom I have trusted, and that he is able to keep that which I have committed to his trust, till the last great rewarding day, when the oppressor and the oppressed, will both stand together and have justice, done by an impartial Judge, who knoweth the secrets of all hearts. God grant that it may be your, and my happy lot, to stand acquitted in that day.

> "This world is all a fleeting show,
> For man's illusion given;
> The smiles of joy, the tears of wo,
> Deceitful shine, deceitful flow;
> Their's nothing true but Heaven."

M. A******

———

THE SUPPLICATION OF ELLEANOR.

Turn, gentle strangers! pass not by in coldness, or in scorn;
Though YE are WHITE; no evil star hung o'er, your natal morn.
In beauty, and in pleasantness, your lives are passing by,
Encircled with rich blessings, with affections pure and high.
O, pause, and listen to my tale; for mercy's tears are sweet.
And blessed is the intercourse, when Love and suffering meet.

   My grandsire was an African—a chieftan in his land;
And the rich earth abundance gave beneath his fostering hand.
At eventide he sat him down beneath his sheltering tree,
And blessed his smiling children with the kind words of the free.
No care oppressed—no evil came—to mar his happy lot;
But full-armed Plenty brought her gifts to his vine-shadowed cot.
The orange and the hyacinth gave him their richest bloom;
While his wide-spread masanga fields poured forth their sweet
        perfumes
Like breathings from the Land of Hope, the harvest promise came,
While all his pleasant vales were bright with flowers without a name.
The hallowed TREE OF WORSHIP stood, with its green vesture on;
And all that dwelt within its shadow blessed the dark Mironne,
Then clustering blessings caught his eye, and rose on every side—
How happy was my grandsire's heart at pleasant even-tide!
But, like an evil ocean-bird, stole nigh the stranger's barque:
And 'neath the shadow of its wings, that smiling scene grew dark!
Lured by the white man's promises, my grandsire left the strand;
And never more did he return to bless his native land!
His wife and weeping little ones, in vain he tried to save!
The chain was fastened on his limbs—and he became a slave.—
No tongue can tell—no heart conceive—how deep that misery stung;
Nor how within his struggling breast the tortured nerves were wrung!
Himself—his wife—his children—stood within the brutal mart;
And, as the hammer coldly fell, the iron reached his heart!
He died—and to those children left a heritage of wrongs;
And well that title, as his heir, to Elleanor belongs.

My mother was of that dark race who owned this noble land,
Before its waving forests bowed beneath the Yengees' hand:
Free as the stirring winds they breathed—unconquered—bold and
   true—
Her fathers to the Council fire their gathering thousands drew.
Strong as the wrath of ocean storm awoke their curbless ire;
And as the lightning from the cloud burst forth its hidden fire!
They knew no tyrant—feared no foe—their ardent souls were free
As their own Narragansett waves, that sang of Liberty.
When first your noble FOUNDER here a pleading outcast came,
The "milk of human kindness" quenched their wrathful spirits' flame—
No more abroad, a wanderer, was he compelled to go;
For he was folded to the breast of MIANTONOMO.
And great CANONICUS sustained the exile's drooping head:
And when your fathers famished here, my fathers gave them bread.
The sad reverse I hasten by. The mighty are laid low,
And o'er their dark, unhonored graves the feet of strangers go.

 The trump of liberty awoke. My father caught the sound;
And though the heavy chain had bent his body to the ground,
His soul responded to the call! His heart awoke again!
And every fibre echoed back fair Freedom's magic strain!
He felt within his bosom, throb the strong pulse of the Free,
When Hope to his entranc-ed ear had whispered—"Liberty!"
No peril had the power to daunt—no suffering to dismay,
So that the iron chain no more upon his bosom lay.
What could he lose! He nothing had but a poor, passing breath—
Away he hied, to win the prize of Liberty—or death—
When terror, with a palsying touch, through other bosoms ran,
He nobly battled for the right—TO CALL HIMSELF A MAN!
He struggled—labored—suffered—with a still unquailing heart,
Until our groaning country saw her hostile foes depart.—
And what was his reward, who toiled so long and ardently?
The STOLEN GEM was given back—the slave again was free.
From ocean to far ocean now, through all our glorious land,
The pinions of fair Liberty in beauteous light expand!

O will ye not remember when, bright flashing to the brim,
The cup of blessing runneth o'er, to give one thought to HIM?
My father toiled—my father bled—these blessings to obtain;
But for the rights which YE possess, his children cry in vain!
Wronged—persecuted—driven forth—behold, alone I stand,
An alien, here, amid the light of my own native land!
Alone! Ah! not alone, thank God! there are a noble few,
Who understand and yield the claims, to truth and justice due!
Kind Ladies! on your every head, a blessing pure I crave;
For when I sank, discouraged—lone—your hands were stretched to
        save!
O be the skies that bend above you, ever calm and fair;
And never may your lips pour forth one poor unanswered prayer!
May your Lives be a Book of Love where kindliest things are writ;
And all affection's dearest bonds around them closely knit.
May all your daughters be like gems in richest casket set;
Your sons like noble pillars in some lofty palace met.
I cannot speak the thoughts I feel—my words are poor and rude;
But in this bosom ever lives the light of gratitude.
O, may our Heavenly Father still his choicest blessings send;
Above you may the hallowed skies in gladness ever bend!
The INDIAN current of my blood, is living with the thought
Of all the kind regard and care, which money never taught!
Deep is the memory of love, within my bosom set,
And its true NARRAGANSETT chords will never—ne'er—forget!

F. H. W.

Providence, Nov. 7 1838.

———

THE EMANCIPATED.

The queenly daughter of a mighty prince,
Ellura, woke to being—nursed and loved
With such a doating tenderness, that all
Which she but *seemed* to wish—or hoped *might* be—
Was done.—And she was lovely. —Genius

Had set upon her ebon brow his seal—
And breathed into her soul—and filled her eye
With the rich fulness of his living light.—
She read the book of Nature.—Stars and clouds,
The glorious sun—the calm and gentle moon—
The cloud-capt mountain brow—vale, fount, and stream—
The broad expanse of ocean, calm and still—
Or lashed anon by tempests—The blue sky,
In its serene repose—The song of birds—
The painted cup of flower or insect-wing—
The lightning's quivering flash, and vivid gleam;
The awful voice that spake from thunder clouds;
Were things familiar when she saw, and heard,
The mysteries of living poesy.—
Nor these alone—the simplest things were fraught
With interests, such as Genius, only, gives
To objects oft beheld. The common light—
A broken shell—the voice and wondrous touch
Of the invisible wind—pebbles, and grass,
And insects—yea, the very sands she trode—
Were marked as wonders.

                Thus Ellura grew—
Delicate as the mimosa tree that sprang
Within her father's kraal. Gleesome, too,
And fleet and graceful as the young spring-bok
That fed from her soft hand. As a bright star
That shineth, singly, o'er the lone midnight,
So shone Ellura o'er the darkend soul
Of her tyrannic father. He—the king
Whose every word was law—whose will was death—
Whose very life, repeated miracle—
Was led and governed, though he recked it not,
By the sweet graces of his gentle child.
She was his light of life—his joy—his pride—
An oasis within his desert arms.
Her dream of life passed on—a dream it was—
For nought within reality's dark sphere

Could match its fervid beauty.
                       One mild eve—
Ellura walked, as it had been her wont,
Along the breezy shore. The murmuring waves
Had come, with their sweet music, to her feet,
Winning her ready ear. The glorious stars
Drew upward her dark eye, that turned above,
With love as purely fervent, as she knew
Her soul had found its kindred spirits there.

And so profound her reverie was, a keel
Of stranger barque touched lightly the smooth strand
Ere she was fairly roused. And when there sprang
From thence a youth of gentle air and mien,
Ellura would have fled;—but first she stole
One truant look—and something—she scarce knew,
Or why—or whence—told her there could not be
Or wrong—or danger—just to speak one word
Of kindness to the stranger. So she paused—
Modest in Nature's pure simplicity—
And when the youth drew nigh, she bade him go.
And she would give him food and resting-place
Beneath her father's roof-tree. Wondering,
He took the gentle hand that was held out,
With a sweet, modest, hospitable air:—
And so Ellura led the stranger youth
Unto the dwelling of her tyrant sire.

Three days he tarried. Then, with courteous speech
Of many thanks, and promise of return—
He knelt before the monarch, and received
His parting words of blessing—kissed the brow
Of wondering Ellura—bade farewell:—
And, followed by the single-hearted sons
Of simple Africa, he parted thence.

Again 'twas eve—calm, silent, glorious eve!—
"Why doth he linger?" These few words were breathed

As low and plaintive as the sorrowing wind,
That, sighing, hovers o'er the few bright flowers—
Low murmuring tenderly—when it hath come
To bid farewell to Summer;—and a girl
Passed from within the shadow of a rock,
And stood alone upon th' untrodden beach
Of Western Africa.

               Her jewelled arms
Were lifted—and her hands were firmly clasped
A moment, and her eye had scanned the waves—
It caught no trace of barque or coming sail
Upon the far blue ocean; and her ear
Was bent intently; but it met no sound
Of waters gurgling at the dip of oar.
Ah! generous, trusting, simple-hearted girl!
Thou waitest, fondly, an expected guest—
The stranger youth is that expected one—
With a desponding thought she turned away
From the wide sea whose calmness mocked her hopes.
A thin, transparent haze hung o'er the sky,
Like gentle melancholy visible—
Orion's coronet shone liquidly—
And the sweet Pleiades were looking down,
With sorrowing lustre, as if tear-drops shone
With each starry eye—tears for the lost—
Their unforgotten sister who had gone,
Of erst, *their* way of glory, making full
The circlet of their harmony. A strange,
Yet sweet profound of stillness hushed the scene—
Ocean breathed quietly as if he dreamed—
And the wild sea-bird scarcely dipped her wing
As, hovering an instant o'er the deep,
She listened, pleased—then found her wave girt nest,
    A dashing oar—a step—Ellura heard
A moment—and th' embedying of her dreams
Stood visibly before her. One short cry
Of joyful recognition; and her heart

Was all too full for words. With gallant air
The stranger greeted her. Then, with fair words
That spake of many wonders, he had drawn
The simple, kind, confiding, gentle one
To visit his fair barque.

                            With a firm step
She went—the fond, devoted, generous girl—
And left her native land—forever left
Her father's tender arms—home—happiness—
And liberty. She turned to him whose eye
Had been to her a new-found sun, and knelt—
And prayed that he might take her back again
Unto her father. Then she clasped his knees,
With many tears, and looked up in his face
With such appealing confidence that aught
But stone had melted. But one icy look—
One mocking word—one cruel, cold repulse—
And, then, the *chain!* Was there no other hand
Than thine, thou wretch! to clench that chain? Or would
Thy dainty villainy do more than kill?

    The horrid truth burst quick upon her mind—
And she was crushed. Withering at once, she felt
The cruel pangs of death without its peace!
Then on her soul a heavy torpor fell—
And dark as heavy—without fear or hope—
Or sense of pain—or thought of the cold chains
That hung upon her limbs, or of the heaps
Of fettered wretches. Speechless—tearless—cold—
Breathing, yet living not—she saw the shore
Recede till it was vanished. One wild shriek
Burst from her cold, blue lips! She tore her hair!
And wrung her fettered, bleeding, helpless hands!
Then—madness crowned the work of treachery!

                        Two long years
Had gone since poor Ellura was a slave—

Since, bought and sold, she wore the fettered limb.
Returning reason had but served to make
The captive more a captive, and perfect
The work of wretchedness. But when she stood,
One pleasant night, with eye bent o'er the sea,
Whose other shore was her own native land—
And faithful Memory brought each dear loved scene,
A flood of tears, which long had frozen round
Her icy heart, gushed upward:—and she wept—
For Slavery had bound her very tears—
But now they were unchained.

              With a calm brow
She knelt upon the strand; and, with deep faith,
Prayed for deliverance—nor prayed in vain—
The sound of coming steps—a fearful cry—
Ellura sprang upon her feet—when lo!—
A wan, wild, haggard, hoary-headed man,
With outstretched arms whence broken fetters hung,
Clasped her unto his bosom! one low cry
Escaped her fixing lips—"My father! Oh!
My father!"—and she sank within his arms,
A breathless, senseless weight. "They come! They come!!"
He cried; and grasping her, with lightning speed
He reached a jutting cliff—triumphant turned
A look on his pursuers—sprang below,
With a wild shout, into the friendly deep,
That oped her arms and met him like a friend.

   The craven ones who followed, struck with awe,
Stood, palsied, on the beach. Anon two forms
Hovered an instant o'er the yawning waves—
And like the billow's swell a voice came up—
"To liberty—To liberty!—We're free!!"

                            F. H. W.

FINIS.

Appendices
to the 2014 Edition

WE, the undersigned, having known and employed Elleanor Eldridge to work for us during many years, recommend her as an uncommonly industrious woman—honest and faithful. We think her deserving to hold the property so dearly bought, with the hard labor of thirty years; and worthy a PREMIUM for her untiring

perseverance to make herself independent of charity, when sickness, or old age should disable her to pursue her accustomed avocations.

Anna Arnold,
Anna Lockwood,
Amey A. Arnold,
Mrs. Elizabeth Elliot,
Mrs. W. Rhodes,
A. T. Lockwood,
D. B. Lockwood,
Mrs. E. G. Chandler,
Mary T. Gladding,
Mrs. H. Chandler,
Mrs. H. Cushing.

MEMOIRS OF ELLEANOR ELDRIDGE.—A small volume, with the above title, has been left on our table. It purports to be the history of the person whose name appears in the title page. From a hasty glance at the book, we learn that Elleanor is a colored woman residing in Providence, R. I., that she accumulated a small property, amounting to some two or three thousand dollars by her own industry, and was eventually wronged out of the whole of it. The book was written by a friend with a view to assist the unfortunate woman in her embarrassments. Price 25 cents. For sale at the Anti Slavery Depository.

Top: Appendix A. Women of Rhode Island who endorsed Eldridge's *Memoirs* in 1838.
Bottom: Appendix B. Advertisement for and review of *Memoirs of Elleanor Eldridge* in the *Christian Secretary*, April 6, 1848.

By purchasing a copy of this little book, and interesting ourselves to promote its sale, we shall be practically illustrating the great duty which Christ enjoined—" doing unto others as we would that they should do unto us :" and the blessing of one grateful heart, at least, shall be ours. Let us, then, as many as are a-ble, purchase her book ; and, on all suitable occasions, recommend it to the purchase of others.

HARRIET LEE TRUESDELL,
FRANCES HARRIET WHIPPLE,
MRS. ELIZABETH G. CHANDLER
MRS. AMEY A. ARNOLD,
MRS. MARY A. EARLE,
MRS. HARRIET CHANDLER,
MRS. ABBY THURBER,
MRS. SARAH OLNEY,
ELIZABETH ELLIOT,
A. G. DORRANCE,
MRS. ANNE ARNOLD.

Appendix C . Women of Rhode Island who endorsed *Elleanor's Second Book.* Overleaf: Appendix D. Title page of *List of Persons Assessed in the Town-Tax . . . of Providence, June 1830,* and page listing "People of Colour." (Images courtesy of the American Antiquarian Society)

Providence

A

LIST OF PERSONS ASSESSED

IN THE

TOWN-TAX

OF

THIRTY-FIVE THOUSAND DOLLARS,

VOTED BY THE FREEMEN OF PROVIDENCE.

JUNE, 1830.

WITH THE AMOUNT OF VALUATION

AND TAX OF EACH.

PROVIDENCE:
PRINTED AND PUBLISHED BY HUTCHENS & WEEDEN.
::::::::::::::::::
1830.

NAMES.	Real.	Tax on Real.
Smith Abby and Clairmont Thayer	7	2,13¼
Slater Samuel for the Peddy Bowen est.	250	76,25
Sessions Harvey	7	2,13¼
Steere Wanton heirs' est.	33	10,06½
Stone Henry N. Providence	6	1,83
Searle Sarah	13	3,96¾
Stillwell Daniel	4	1,22
Snelling Samuel Jr.	4	1,22
Thompson Ebenezer	7	2,13½
Taylor Peter G. New-York	26	7,93
Valentine Henry	24	7,32
Waterman Elisha	20	6,10
Waterman Richard	42	12,81
Waterman George	2	,61
Waterman John	12	3,66
Walcott Lewis and Jabez heirs' est. Cumberland	11	3,35½
Whipple Thomas	16	4,88
Whipple Simon heirs' est.	9	2,74½
Williams Caleb Cranston	4	1,22
Wild Rebecca widow, Hartford	36	10,98
Do. do. " for Henry Grew children est.	36	
Wanton Joseph heirs' est for water lot No. 9 and house		10,98
lot No. 13 on Abbot's Plat	9	2,74½
Wetmore William S. Lima S. A.	70	21,35
Walker Appleton New-York	3	,91½
Wetmore Thomas Boston for James Arnold est.	45	13,72½

PEOPLE OF COLOUR.

Barnes Edward	12	3,66
Brunel and Joseph Case and wife est.	4	1,22
Brown Jenny	3	,91½
Bowen Isaac	4	1,22
Taber Henry heirs' est.	3	,91½
Willis George	5	1,52½
Cozzens Richard heirs' est.	5	1,52½
Congdon Hodge	6	1,83
Waterman George and O. Tibbitts	5	1,52½
Ceazer Oliver Smith	6	1,83
Rosario Jacob heirs' est.	10	3,05
Daniels John	2	,61
Phenix John O.	1	,30½
Ellis James E.	5	1,52½
Essex Thomas	8	2,44
Ellen Eldred	6	1,83
Nigar Alfred	7	2,13½
Gibbs Abraham est.	3	,91½
Gross William A.	1	,30½
Haskell George	3	,91½
Haskell Charles (lives with T. Rivers)	7	2,13½
Harris James heirs' est.	6	1,83
Hammond Thomas heirs' est.	6	1,83
Haskell Benjamin New-Haven	3	,91½
Jones Rosanna	18	5,49
Lewis Philip Barber	18	5,49
Roberts Reuben	2	,61
Martin Henry	3	,91½
M'Carty George	5	1,52½
Northup Ichabod	3	,91½
Tillinghast Michael	12	3,66

About the Authors

Joycelyn K. Moody is the Sue E. Denman Distinguished Chair in American Literature and Professor of English at the University of Texas at San Antonio, where she teaches and publishes on black print culture studies, US narratives of slavery, African American autobiography, and women's self-representation. She is also founding Director of UTSA's African American Literatures and Cultures Institute. With John Ernest, she coedits the West Virginia University Press series *Regenerations: African American Literature and Culture*.

Elleanor Eldridge (b. 1785–d. 1862), a woman of African and indigenous descent, was born free in Rhode Island. She and her siblings acquired considerable property and local prestige, despite rampant racism against people of color in the state. As a successful proprietor and entrepreneur in Warwick and Providence, Elleanor Eldridge cultivated and maintained harmonious relationships with the white women she served such that they backed her during a series of lawsuits in which she was involved, and eventually won.

Frances Harriet Whipple Green McDougall (b. 1805–d. 1878) was a minor US woman writer committed to developing a career for herself as a publishing social activist as well as to creating opportunities for other women and for people of color. Her first publication, *The Original,* was a short-lived early 1820s magazine for New England women. Her biographies of Elleanor Eldridge followed. She went on to publish in multiple genres ranging from abolitionist magazines, to prolabor tracts, botany textbooks, and temperance and Spiritualist tracts.

CPSIA information can be obtained at www.ICGtesting.com
Printed in the USA
LVOW11s0322211015

459078LV00001B/26/P

9 781935 978237